Library of
Davidson College

The Poetry and Poetics of Jorge Luis Borges

American University Studies

Series II
Romance Languages and Literature
Vol. 44

PETER LANG
New York · Berne · Frankfurt am Main

Paul Cheselka

THE POETRY AND POETICS OF JORGE LUIS BORGES

PETER LANG
New York · Berne · Frankfurt am Main

Library of Congress Cataloging-in-Publication Data

Cheselka, Paul.
　　The Poetry and Poetics of Jorge Luis Borges.

　　(American University Studies. Series II,
Romance Languages and Literature ; vol. 44)
　　　Bibliography: p.
　　　1. Borges, Jorge Luis, 1899 – 1986 – Poetic works.
I. Title.　II. Series.
PQ7797.B635Z65　　1987　　　861　　　86-18922
ISBN 0-8204-0318-0
ISSN 0740-9257

CIP-Kurztitelaufnahme der Deutschen Bibliothek

Cheselka, Paul:
The Poetry and Poetics of Jorge Luis Borges /
Paul Cheselka. -- New York ; Berne ; Frankfurt
am Main : Lang, 1987.
　　(American University Studies : Ser. 2,
　　Romance Languages and Literature ; Vol. 44)
　　ISBN 0-8204-0318-0

NE: American University Studies / 02

© Peter Lang Publishing, Inc., New York 1987

All rights reserved.
Reprint or reproduction, even partially, in all forms such as
microfilm, xerography, microfiche, microcard, offset strictly prohibited.

Printed by Weihert-Druck GmbH, Darmstadt (West Germany)

Borges cree que la poesía es álgebra y fuego. Reconozco mi deuda al "álgebra" de Carlos Bousoño y al "fuego" de José Luis Cano. De forma análoga, les agradezco a otros de mis maestros—a George Wing, a Carter Wheelock, y a Ricardo Gullón.

* * *

Toutes choses sont dites déjà, mais comme personne n'écoute il faut toujours recommencer.—André Gide.

Contents

	Page
Introduction	1
Chapter 1: Borges and the Art of Poetry	7
Chapter 2: Prelude to Fervor	23
Chapter 3: Buenos Aires Fervor	49
Chapter 4: Moon Across the Way	87
Chapter 5: A San Martín Notebook	107
Chapter 6: The Myth of the "Lyrical Hiatus" 1930–1960	121
Chapter 7: The Maker's World	149
Chapter 8: Borges' Poetry 1960–1964	171
Conclusion	189
A Selected Bibliography	195

Introduction

Horacio Jorge Becco's *Jorge Luis Borges Bibliografía total 1923–1973* lists over one thousand bibliographical items on Borges, and in the decade since its publication, dozens of additional items have appeared in print each year. Much of the early criticism is polemical in nature: Borges' detractors vilify him while his supporters eulogize him. In María Luisa Bastos' book *Borges ante la crítica argentina 1923–1960*, the polemical rather than purely literary tone of much of the criticism is obvious. Indeed, perhaps with the exception of Ana María Barrenechea's *La expresión de la irrealidad en la obra de Jorge Luis Borges* (first published in 1957), there is relatively little enlightening literary criticism on Borges before the 1960's. Thus, in 1968, when Ronald Christ wrote his "Preface" to *The Narrow Act: Borges' Art of Allusion*, he was able to state:

> There is no longer any need for introducing Borges to the English-speaking world or for justifying a study of his fiction—perhaps only a necessity for explaining why such a study has not already been undertaken. At any rate, no such book-length study was available when I began my work some years ago, and at the time of writing this preface no such work is yet available despite Paul de Man's statement in his 1964 review, "A Modern Master": "American and English critics have called him [Borges] one of the greatest writers alive today, but have not yet (so far as I know) made substantial contributions to the interpretation of his works."[1]

Fortunately, this deficiency has been largely corrected by the appearance of an abundance of quality criticism in the last decade and a half, that has extensively covered many aspects of Borges' prose fiction. Nevertheless, Christ's statement remains as accurate as it was in 1968 if it is applied to Borges' poetry. Although Borges launched his literary career as a poet, the overwhelming majority of literary critics have chosen to ignore this aspect of the writer's work. André Maurois' "Preface" to *Labyrinths: Selected Stories and Other Writings* (published in 1962) is typical of this tendency to ignore the very existence of Borges' poetry; the first sentence of Maurois' "Preface" reads as follows: "Jorge Luis Borges is a great writer who has composed only little essays or short narratives."[2] The tendency to ignore Borges' poetry still persists in the 1980's. Gene H. Bell-Villada, in his generally sensible study of Borges' prose fiction (*Borges and His Fiction*, published in 1981), summarily dismisses Borges' poetry with this brief comment:

> Though unmistakeable in its voice and its moods, and often times moving and quite beautiful, Borges's poetry is mostly of local and therefore secondary interest; he is a very good poet, if not a great one.[3]

Bell-Villada's comments seem to be a faint echo of Néstor Ibarra's 1930 views of some of the shortcomings of Borges' poetry (Ibarra faults it for its "sistemático localismo") rather than a representation of a fresh perspective on the subject.[4] Since Borges' first three poetry collections contain in embryonic form virtually all of the motifs, themes, and preoccupations that many years later would be used to help weave the author's short stories, one can only suppose that critics will do well to study, along with Borges' prose, the poetry that preceded it.

A result of past neglect is that there are still only two full-length studies dedicated to Borges' poetry that merit attention. The first of these—Guillermo Sucre's *Borges, el poeta*—originally appeared in 1967; Donald Yates gives the following assessment of Sucre's work:

> El libro de Sucre es el primero en acometer un extenso examen del desarrollo de Borges como poeta. Si su estudio es inteligente, elaborado con ideas personales y simpatía, carece por otro lado de un método crítico formal y, a fin de cuentas, no revela ningún aspecto nuevo de la poesía de Borges, ninguna interpretación original del espíritu poético del autor.[5]

The major problem with Sucre's study is that it lacks a clear focus, and thus the different chapters do not form a cohesive, logical, overall view of Borges' poetry.

The other full-length study of Borges' poetry is Zunilda Gertel's *Borges y su retorno a la poesía* that was co-published in 1969 by the University of Iowa and Las Américas Publishing Company. While Gertel does spend considerable time speculating and theorizing about why Borges increased his level of poetic activity in the 1950's, she spends relatively little time discussing the poetry representing Borges' supposed "return" to poetry. The book studies the poetry up until 1964 and is divided into three chapters followed by a very brief conclusion. The first chapter speaks of Borges' increasing literary fame, reviews the existing criticism of Borges' work up until the middle of the 1960's, and presents Gertel's purpose in writing the work; Gertel sums it up as follows:

> Creemos poder demostrar una razón más profunda del retorno a la poesía en el hallazgo del símbolo personal o "privado", elemento conductor de la inquietud metafísica que el poeta no logró expresar en su época ultraísta.[6]

In a nutshell, Gertel believes that Borges' poetry before the 1960 publication of *El hacedor* was somehow deficient and represented a prolonged search for Borges' own "private symbol." Gertel maintains that the poet discovered this symbol in the late 1950's (the symbol represents the harmonious resolution of clashing opposites); she believes that this symbol explains Borges' increased publication of poems. Gertel also feels that the discovery of his "private symbol" allowed the poet to write his finest, best realized works, attaining what Gertel calls "la plenitud de la creación borgiana."[7] Nevertheless, Gertel devotes only one chapter—"Función de los principios poéticos en el verso"—to actual study of Borges' poems. Most of this chapter is devoted to Borges' first three poetry collections, and to analyzing the poems Borges wrote during his so-called "lyrical hiatus" when he was supposedly not writing very much poetry; only a few scant pages deal with the new poems contained in *El hacedor* and *Obra poética 1923-1964*. Gertel's arguments are weakened by the fact that of the fifty-eight "new" poems contained in these two works, she only mentions or attempts an analysis of five texts to illustrate and to prove her basic premise: that Borges' "new" poetry is somehow superior to his previous work because of his discovery of his "personal symbol." Gertel fails to provide convincing proof to show how the mere fact of possessing a "personal symbol" makes Borges' poetry any better than it was before. In addition, it is open to debate whether this "personal symbol" came to the forefront in the late 1950's as Gertel maintains, or if it is already present in Borges' poems back in the 1920's.

The most valuable part of Gertel's study is the second (and longest) chapter entitled "La teoría poética de Borges"; in it she delineates with a good deal of skill Borges' fundamental ideas and beliefs about poetry as expressed not in his poetry, but rather in his essays. In summary, Gertel's work is valuable as a study of Borges' esthetics as expressed in his prose writings; its chief defect is its failure to address the poetry more forthrightly and in more detail.

Thus, the critic of Borges' poetry has the privilege of being able to study a major portion of an internationally famous author's work without the constraints imposed by the existence of a vigorous critical tradition. It is in this context that the current study of Borges' poetry was born. It is meant to be a basic work that systematically presents the salient events and forces that have shaped Borges' poetic career, and most importantly it is the first study of its kind to deal with large numbers of the poems themselves. This study pretends to be neither complete nor exhaustive, for it emphasizes Borges' poetic theory and themes while delving into other aspects of the poetry in less detail. It limits itself to studying Borges' poetry from his first ultraist poems published in Spain to the publication of *Obra poética 1923-1964*. The substantial number of poems that Borges has written after 1964 will require yet another full-length study to be undertaken in the future either by this or some other critic. By addressing in some fashion all of the one hundred forty-three poems contained in *Obra poética 1923–1964*, I hope to provide a coherent "reader's guide" to a major portion of Borges' poetry. The study does not pretend to travel all the paths or to "explain" Borges' poetry; its purpose is to help the reader *experience* the texts.

The poems from each segment of Borges' poetic trajectory are divided into thematic groups and then methodically analyzed. The goal of the many separate analyses is to help the texts finally speak for themselves as much as possible; the recurring patterns in the analyses can then be used to forge an overall synthesis of Borges' poetic world. In a sense the critical method used here mimics the method Borges himself uses in the poems: the repeated presentation of a limited number of essential themes with greater and lesser variations. The seemingly redundant patterns produce unity and greater clarity, through the constantly shifting hues of nuance. Although none of Borges' individual poems is *the* poem that the poet seeks to write, a series of poems on the same theme taken as a group approach the archetypal perfection to which the poet ardently aspires but wisely resigns himself to never attaining. In short, this study tries to aid the reader to develop his or her own appreciation of the poems, and is meant to be read along with the poems and not as a distant critical commentary. Borges, speaking as one who knows critical readers, has said: "Los alumnos piden generalmente bibliografías . . . pero yo les digo que no hay nada mejor que el texto mismo."[8]

Notes

[1] Ronald J. Christ, *The Narrow Act: Borges' Art of Allusion* (New York: New York University Press), p. xi.

[2] Jorge Luis Borges, *Labyrinths: Selected Stories and Other Writings*, Donald A. Yates and James Irby editors, "Preface" by André Maurois (Norfolk, Connecticut: New Directions Books, 1962), p. ix.

[3] Gene H. Bell-Villada, *Borges and His Fiction. A Guide to His Mind and Art* (Chapel Hill, N.C.: The University of North Carolina Press, 1981), p. xii.

[4] María Luisa Bastos, *Borges ante la crítica argentina* (Buenos Aires: Ediciones Hispamerica, 1974), p. 45–46.

[5] Donald A. Yates, "Cinco años de crítica borgiana: 13 libros nuevos," *Jorge Luis*

Borges: El escritor y la crítica, Jaime Alazraki, editor (Madrid: Taurus Ediciones, 1976), p. 298.

[6] Zunilda Gertel, *Borges y su retorno a la poesía*. (New York: The University of Iowa and Las Américas Publishing Co., 1969), p. 31.

[7] Gertel, p. 31.

[8] M.P. Montecchia, *Reportaje a Borges* (Buenos Aires: Ediciones Crisol, 1977), p. 12.

1

Borges and the Art of Poetry

Within the confines of the western literary tradition, one important function of poetry is to help remedy the inadequacies of the language of ordinary discourse. The principal inadequacy of ordinary language stems from the fact that the unique psychic intuitions of one human being are not directly and identically transmissible to another human being. Poetry helps to fill this void by providing a highly charged form of language capable of producing the illusion of faithfully reproducing the psychic intuitions of one individual in the mind of another. For a poem to exist the reader must willingly suspend belief in the objective reality that the exact duplication of psychic intuitions is impossible; thus, as preconditions the reader must know that the text is to be read, and mentally received as a poem, and must be prepared to enter the poem's specialized world of illusion. These thoughts are summarized in Carlos Bousoño's concise definition of the poetic process:

> Nuestra inicial afirmación será esta: la poesía debe darnos la impresión (aunque esa impresión puede ser engañosa) de que, a través de meras palabras, se nos comunica un conocimiento de muy especial índole: el conocimiento de un contenido psíquico *tal como un contenido psíquico es en la vida real*. O sea, de un contenido psíquico que en la vida real se ofrece como algo individual, como un todo particular, síntesis intuitiva, única, de lo conceptual-sensorial-afectivo.[1]

Therefore, what poetry actually communicates is not the original intuition itself—which is impossible—but rather the contemplation or the recreation of that intuition. In this manner, the reader or hearer of the poem in a sense becomes the co-author of the poem, for the poem truly exists only in the

7

rekindling of the poetic intuition. Bousoño also stipulates another condition for the existence of poetry—each hearing or reading of the poem should produce an esthetic joy or pleasure, without which the poem is lifeless. Bousoño believes that this "joy" comes from "la sensación de plenitud vital que experimentamos al perfeccionarnos conociendo" (CB p. 20). Jorge Luis Borges strongly believes in both the co-authorship concept of the poem and in the importance of the realization of esthetic pleasure. In his "Prólogo" to *Obra poética 1923–1964* he states:

> . . . la poesía está en el comercio del poema con el lector, no en la serie de símbolos que registran las páginas de un libro. Lo esencial es el hecho estético, el *thrill*, la modificación física que suscita cada lectura. Esto acaso no es nuevo; pero a mis años las novedades importan menos que la verdad.[2]

Robert Scholes in his book *Structuralism in Literature* sheds additional light on poetry's special function:

> It is as if the poet in the process of making a true poem turns on some additional neural circuitry which enables him to produce these high-powered verbal objects called poems. The result, in Saussurean terms, is that the poet's utterance (*parole*) comes from a different sign-system (*langue*) than employed by an ordinary speaker.[3]

Although, technically speaking, poetic language can exist outside of the literary genre called poetry, in practice the poetic language loses much of its necessary intensity if it is taken as prose or as ordinary conversation. Therefore, the difference between the expressiveness of ordinary language and that of the poem is quantitative—the intuitions communicated by poems are denser and more complex. The reader accepts the poem's added complexity as a necessity born out of poetry's special mission to explore complex realities, whereas the reader does not accept this level of language in the form of prose or ordinary conversation where simpler realities require a simpler level of language.

Scholes describes the nature of the special type of communication to which poetry aspires as follows:

> Poetry, in fact, was shrewdly defined by John Stuart Mill as an utterance which is not heard but overheard. The point of this is that poetry may be definable precisely in terms of our having to supply the missing elements in an act of communication. The "fictional" element in literature, including poetry, is definable as an absent context, or perhaps as a distant context. Insofar as a literary work is mimetic it refers to the "real" world by interposing an "imaginary" world between its audience and reality. (RS p. 27–28)

Poetry is historical; therefore, the poems' effectiveness depends on the cultural values of the society they reflect and on the language in which they are written. Individual poems "die" in the sense that they can become "unpoetic." If, with the passage of time, readers can no longer identify with the sentiments, ideas, or values contained in the poem, the text will be labeled as "dated," "inappropriate," or "inadequate"; the poem ceases to be poetry because it has now failed in its basic mission of creating an illusory world in which the reader can simulate within himself the poet's inner world. Moreover, without active reader complicity, there is no poetry. In an anthropological sense, poetry is not always cross-cultural, for what is interpreted as poetic in one society at any given moment, would not necessarily be considered poetic in another society at that same time. In short, poetry is very fragile—it can be destroyed by the flow of history, by the changing cultural values within the same society, or by its inability to cross the cultural lines of other societies. Poetry can also be destroyed by the very language in which it is written because language is a repository of a society's evolving cultural values. As languages evolve, the meanings and connotations of words change, and thus the meanings of poems also are in a constant state of flux. As poetry is largely based on the connotative rather than the denotative power of words, it is clear that a poem written centuries ago must necessarily produce different psychic resonances in the minds of each subsequent generation of readers.

The "great poems" one finds in an anthology spanning many centuries of historical time are the select few works that have somehow managed to withstand the constant permutations of history, culture and language. Another problem that poetry faces is that it is the most difficult literary form to translate into a "foreign" language. Indeed, the word "foreign" is especially appropriate in this context because the translated poem may indeed sound very "foreign" in its new language and cultural context; "good poems" often become "bad poems" in translation.

Given its many fragilities, one might wonder how the literary genre called poetry even manages to survive. Paradoxically one of poetry's greatest strengths is the relative paucity of its themes; poetry has only a few essential themes all of which are commonplace to the point of utter banality. Bousoño flatly states that "el pensamiento en la poesía casi no puede ser otra cosa que un lugar común . . ." (CB p. 24). Simply put, poetry's ultimate banality saves and justifies it by making it universal. Bousoño sums it up as follows: "La poesía es universal porque el pensamiento que en ella reside no es, en postrer esquematización nuevo" (CB p. 24). To survive the passage of time all good poetry must be firmly rooted in the few themes that delve into the immutable qualities of human nature that go beyond culture and history. Poems that depend on novelty—such as those produced by the early twentieth-century avant-garde literary movements—are the first to die; the few "novelty" poems that do survive are considered valuable as historical curiosity pieces. For example, it is indeed ironic that Guillaume Apollinaire is less remembered for his once daring experiments in *Calligrammes* than for one apparently very simple and ordinary poem—"Le Pont Mirabeau"—that revolves about the richly commonplace metaphor of the flowing river as a representation of the flow of time, love, and men's lives. Good poetry is saved by a paradox: its infinitely complex world endures through the ages by dint of its inherent simplicity.

Poetry's simultaneous complexity and simplicity create many

pitfalls for the critic. No one method or approach can ever pretend to exhaust all of a poem's possibilities; Robert Scholes sums up the blind arrogance inherent in any attempt to impose a "definitive" methodology on the study of all poetry:

> . . . nor can any entirely satisfactory method exist without some way of determining the relationships among *all* structures in the poem and *all* responses, conscious and unconscious, in the reader. The impossibility of detecting and evaluating such responses sets limits to the ability of any methodology to settle the value or the meaning of any single poem. The pretense that such limits do not exist is responsible for much of the nonsense uttered by literary critics, whatever their persuasion. (RS p. 27–28)

The most common method used thus far to define Borges' own personal poetics has been to make use of the author's numerous essays on literary topics and esthetics as the principle source of raw material. This method was successfully used by Allen W. Phillips in his article "Borges y su concepto de la metáfora" in which he traces the evolution of Borges' poetic thought with special emphasis on the role of the metaphor. It is especially noteworthy that Phillips limits the period of the "exaltation of the metaphor" to the years 1918–1923. Phillips correctly points out that the original 1923 prologue to *Fervor de Buenos Aires* already clearly shows Borges' disenchantment with the ultraist movement. In this prologue Borges states that he knows that his "sectarian comrades" will consider some of his remarks "blasphemous." Among the blasphemies are a rejection of ultraism's mania for novelty in favor of whatever will work most efficaciously in a given situation, and recognition that there are many valid literary methodologies. Thus, while Borges was busily rejecting ultraism's dogmatic tenets in the prologue and in the actual poems of *Fervor de Buenos Aires*, he simultaneously affirmed his solidarity with the ultraist movement in a piece published in the May 1923 issue of the magazine *Nosotros*. Such clear discrepancies show that as early as 1923, the literary theories Borges seemed to advance in his manifestos and essays were already far behind what he was doing in his poetry.

The facts cast serious doubt on Zunilda Gertel's assertion that Borges' poetic theory is ahead of and largely dictates the content of his poetry; Gertel maintains:

> Los principios analizados nos permiten demostrar que la teoría poética de Borges se adelanta a su creación, en cierto modo la prescribe y explica también sus contradicciones como una necesaria dialéctica.[4]

Based on the poet's essays, Gertel gives 1952 as the year in which Borges "finally" rejects the "new metaphor":

> En esta búsqueda de un nuevo cauce lírico, Borges reconocerá definitivamente, al cabo de tantas dudas y reticencias, en 1952, el fracaso de la metáfora nueva y la necesidad del retorno a las metáforas eternas. (ZG p. 89)

However, the quote Gertel uses as proof really dates from March 1949 when Borges first used that essay—"Nathaniel Hawthorne"—as a part of a lecture series on American literature at the Colegio Libre de Estudios Superiores. Even more telling than this small oversight is that the essay's principal theoretical point—that truly new metaphors cannot be invented and that the few essential metaphors have always existed—was expressed as early as 1925 in *Inquisiciones*. Phillips stresses Borges' early disaffection with the idea of coining new metaphors, labeling the 1924–1928 period as one that shows the poet's disenchantment with ultraist theories. Phillips quotes a key line from *Inquisiciones* which further damages the validity of Gertel's chronology of Borges' poetics. Borges states: "no es dable urdir metáforas de una plenaria novedad."[5] Phillips goes on to point out that this is merely the first formulation of a concept that Borges brings up quite frequently in subsequent texts; the 1949 "Nathaniel Hawthorne" text is a restatement of what Borges believed back in the 1920's and clearly does not represent any radical change in the poet's thought. In the often-quoted "Nathaniel Hawthorne" essay Borges states:

> ... es quizá un error suponer que puedan inventarse metáforas. Las verdaderas, las que formulan íntimas conexiones entre una imagen y

> otra, han existido siempre; las que aún podemos inventar son las falsas, las que no vale la pena inventar.[6]

Borges' 1952 text "La metáfora" that was added to the 1953 edition of *Historia de la eternidad* also sums up his thoughts on the metaphor:

> El primer monumento de las literaturas occidentales, la *Ilíada*, fue compuesto hará tres mil años; es verosímil conjeturar que en ese enorme plazo todas las afinidades íntimas, necesarias (ensueño-vida, sueño-muerte, ríos y vidas que transcurren, etcétera), fueron advertidas y escritas alguna vez. Ello no significa, naturalmente, que se haya agotado el número de metáforas; los modos de indicar o insinuar estas secretas simpatías de los conceptos resultan de hecho, ilimitados.[7]

In an interview with Jean De Milleret, Borges repeats once again his long-held views on the metaphor:

> Ahora creo que las únicas metáforas buenas son los lugares comunes. Porque los lugares comunes corresponden a verdaderas afinidades entre las cosas mientras que las metáforas que se inventan no corresponden a afinidades reales; son arbitrarias. . . . He escrito un artículo donde decía que tal vez las únicas metáforas válidas son, por ejemplo: el tiempo y el río; la vida y el ensueño; la muerte y el sueño; los ojos y las estrellas, *etc.*, y que el resto de las metáforas son ficticias, o sea que no existen sino de una manera verbal pero no para la sensibilidad.[8]

Despite Borges' real interest in the metaphor, as early as 1928 in *El idioma de los argentinos* the poet professes not to know why more stress has been placed on the metaphor than on other equally important rhetorical devices: "La metáfora es una de tantas habilidades retóricas para conseguir énfasis. No sé por qué razón ha de ser puesta sobre las otras" (AP p. 45). The excessive attention given to both the role of ultraism and the metaphor in Borges' career as a poet is really nothing but another tempest in a teapot created largely by the literary critics themselves. Guillermo Sucre agrees:

> Borges apasionado de ultraísmo. Esa pasión de juventud no parece

haber influido en su propia poesía. Borges fue ultraísta más por sentido del juego, de la aventura, que por convicción estética. Al menos su ultraísmo fue sobre todo intelectual y teórico.[9]

It soon becomes apparent that Borges' works show an often surprising disparity between the theories expressed in prose and the actual practice found in the poems. It is important to note that this disparity is greatest during the decade of the 1920's and rapidly decreases thereafter until the theory and practice finally mesh and become virtually one and the same. In the essays of the 1920's Borges toys with many theories—both philosophical and esthetic—because he finds them intellectually stimulating and derives a good deal of pleasure from them. When picking up his pen to write his own created works, however, the youthful Borges felt little obligation to apply dogmatically the theories expressed in his essayistic adventures (Borges clearly states this in his original prologue to *Fervor de Buenos Aires* in 1923, but many critics steadfastly refuse to listen). The use of Borges' essays to define his poetics is a methodology fraught with pitfalls (Phillips' article avoids these pitfalls more successfully whereas Gertel places undue stress on the content of the 1920's essays as an accurate reflection of the poetry). First, the essays are really only a secondary source of information on the writer's poetry because they are objects outside the textual realm of the poems. Second, it is not logical to assume that a writer's abstract literary theories will automatically be put into full practice in his created work. In Borges' particular case, critics who wish to postulate a close correspondence between the author's literary theory and his practice would be well advised to stay on firmer ground by using essays published in the 1940's or later.

Borges has facilitated the study of his poetics by providing a valuable primary source: the poem entitled "Arte poética" published in *El Hacedor* in 1960. This poem is a concise capsule whose semantic content sums up the essential points of Borges' poetic theory while the poem's structure simultaneously illustrates those theories; it is a superb fusion of abstract theory and concrete practice.

Arte Poética

Mirar el río hecho de tiempo y agua
Y recordar que el tiempo es otro río
Saber que nos perdemos como el río
Y que los rostros pasan como el agua.

Sentir que la vigilia es otro sueño
Que sueña no soñar y que la muerte
Que teme nuestra carne es esa muerte
De cada noche, que se llama sueño.

Ver en el día o en el año un símbolo
De los días del hombre y de sus años,
Convertir el ultraje de los años
En una música, un rumor y un símbolo,

Ver en la muerte el sueño, en el ocaso
Un triste oro, tal es la poesía
Que es inmortal y pobre. La poesía
Vuelve como la aurora y el ocaso.

A veces en las tardes una cara
Nos mira desde el fondo de un espejo;
El arte debe ser como ese espejo
Que nos revela nuestra propia cara.

Cuentan que Ulises, harto de prodigios,
Lloró de amor al divisar su Itaca
Verde y humilde. El arte es esa Itaca
De verde eternidad, no de prodigios.

También es como el río interminable
Que pasa y queda y es cristal de un mismo
Heráclito inconstante, que es el mismo
Y es otro, como el río interminable.[10]

In Borges' poetic hierarchy, form is always subordinate to content; the poetry's content dictates the form. Simply stated, the function of form is to maximize the impact of the content. Rather than the method or mechanics of poetry Borges emphasizes the importance of the quality of the communication established with the reader and the overall effect the poem produces upon being read. Form plays an essential role in furthering these ends, but should never be the chief and obvious focus of attention. Thus, in a poem devoted to demonstrating the utter poverty and endless repetition that characterizes all art, the poet chooses a traditional form—the poem is composed of seven quatrains of eleven syllable lines with an a-b-b-a rhyme scheme—to help contribute to the thought that all art is cyclical, ritualistic and repetitive. The idea of literary "poverty" is emphasized by deliberately using the most commonplace metaphors and monotonous rhyme. For example, the rhyme consists of a "mere" repetition of entire words (agua-agua, río-río, sueño-sueño, muerte-muerte, *etc.*). The metaphors chosen are equally "poor": time is a river, death is a dream, identity is revealed in a mirror, and the sunset is compared to a sad gold coin. To complete the idea of cyclical time and cyclical art, the poet uses the last quatrain to summarize the poem's content and to link the poem's end with its beginning (the river imagery provides the immediate physical link): like the art it strives to define the poem itself has become a never ending cycle. Thus, the poem's chief structural artifice is the constant and skillful use of repetition. In short, "Arte poética" is an excellent example of Borges' belief that the function of form is to mimic and thus complement meaning.

A closer analysis of "Arte poética" reveals the poet's overt attempt to realize a harmonious union of form and meaning. The first quatrain presents one of Borges' fundamental intuitions on the basic task of the poet—poets should contemplate, feel, and analyze life in a never-ending search for its true essences. The river metaphor has at least a double meaning; as in Jorge Manrique's "Coplas"—which the river imagery immediately brings to mind—the river symbolizes life's onward flow, but it simultaneously symbolizes the flow of time. Time's river and life's river become one—the substance of human life is linear time. The poet ends the first quatrain recognizing the age old dictum that individual human life is ephemeral, that individuals are reduced to oblivion in the river of time, and that time erases the imprint of individual human identity.

In the second quatrain, Borges replaces the river metaphor with that of life as a dream (here Hispanic literary tradition forces the name of Calderón and his work *La vida es sueño* to mind; the poet is deliberately building on a previous literary tradition). Life is a dream that dreams that it is not dreaming, and the dreams of sleep are nothing but another form of death; the symbols again are meant to be the most commonplace possible. Besides toying with the baroque period's concept of life as a dream, Borges also is presenting his own view that what we call objective reality is actually the ultimate "dream."

In the third quatrain, Borges returns to his attempt to redefine the poet's basic task. First, the poet sees the units used to measure time—days, years—as constant symbolic reminders that time is the substance of man's life and by extension a symbol of his death. The poet's task is to give meaning to "el ultraje de los años" (time's arrogant affront) and to reconcile somehow the conflict caused by time's simultaneous role as man's substance and the force that ultimately destroys him. The poet must seek a justification for man's existence in face of time's reduction of individuals to utter oblivion. Poetry plays the role of arbiter in this reconciliation process in which time's affront is transformed into "una música, un rumor, y un símbolo." These three key words to a large extent define Borges' concept of poetry. The "music" spoken of here (Borges also sees music as a mysterious form of time) is not the euphony Verlaine strove to achieve in the physical sound of the actual verses, but rather this borgesian "music" is composed of communication "waves" by means of which the poet sends out his poetic intuitions to the reader. The music is the medium of communication or structure that bears the message or "rumor." The "rumor"—which suggests whispering—refers to the poetic intuition that the poet desires to communicate; it consists not only of mere information but also of the multiple resonances produced by the "music." The source of both the medium and the cryptic "whispered" message is the muse (the universal consciousness). The meaning of both the "música" and "rumor" is liberated through "símbolo." It is through the effective deciphering of signs and symbols that man can discover and delineate a meaning for his existence.

The fourth quatrain serves to develop more fully Borges' concept of the function of poetry. Poems should retrace already well-trodden paths rather than create new ones; poetry's immortality stems from this essential poverty. Poetry's mission is to see the truth, to see the few essential things that previous generations of poets have already seen and written about, and to seek order in the chaos of the universe. For this reason both poetry's metaphors and its themes must constantly repeat themselves. Just as the themes and metaphors form cyclical, ritualistic patterns, poetry itself is cyclical and ritualistic; poetry is as immortal as the cyclical time of sunrise and sunset. As long as there are human beings there will be poetry, because the desire for "poetic experience" is a basic human drive whose source is to be found in the immutable essences that make up human nature. In this sense, poetry is a "closed" genre in which cyclical time—a counterpart to the cyclical poetry itself—imposes order upon the infinite chaos of the universe.

In the fifth quatrain Borges uses another traditional metaphor: that of art as a mirror that reflects man and his reality. However, art is a mirror not in the sense that it should be a faithful photographic-like reproduction of objective reality, but rather art is a mirror through which man can catch a glimpse of the deepest and most hidden regions of his very being—the mirror of art reflects transcendental, eternal truths. The symbolic mirror of art shows man the road to truth and thus serves as a guide, whereas the real mirrors in Borges' world are symbols of chaos that only serve to remind man of and then to multiply the most disagreeable aspects of reality; the real mirrors also serve to confuse hopelessly the world of reality and illusion. In this manner the poem (art) becomes a form of knowledge, a type of self-contained truth. Through poetry both the poet and the reader seek their own most authentic selves; the poem is a route to greater self-knowledge and a way to see oneself from a fresh perspective. Nonetheless, the mirror of art carries the reflection of man's and art's ultimate failure by showing their myriad imperfections: man's imperfect art serves as a constant reminder of the impossibility of his own total perfection. In short, art is the mirror in which man seeks to discover his own true identity, his roots, his essence, and his destiny.

No new material is presented in the sixth and seventh quatrains; their function is to summarize and reiterate what has already been stated and to draw the last arc to close the poem's circular structure. The sixth quatrain has the added function of introducing a mythical dimension; poetry—like myth—is timeless, and therefore eternal. Myth is important to the poet because it is useful in his search for the essences of things; in myth the poet finds the archetypes that reveal absolute truths and the ideal forms of both people and things. Through the use of myth the poet seeks to recapture briefly the idealized freshness of the first "I" and the perfection of the first rose. The sixth quatrain's intuition is simple: man should cry with love upon contemplating art—which always appears "green" and "humble." Art as a symbol of the essential always seems fresh, new, and pure despite its ancient roots in eternity. When men are tired of "prodigios"—which can symbolize man's absorption into objective reality's daily cares—he seeks refuge in art. Art serves as a protecting "mother," a guardian of the treasure of eternal values. The negation of the word "prodigios" also carries out the function of repeating Borges' idea that art should not attempt to be surprising, original, or "new," as this contradicts art's fundamental purpose which is to serve as a timeless space that contains the immutable essences of man. Once again Borges refutes the basic premises of the avant-garde literary movements; according to the borgesian view of art, the early twentieth-century avant-garde movements failed precisely because of their desire to create new or original worlds—an impossible and senseless task given the fact that all that is essential to both man and his art already exists and has always existed. Therefore, the function of the poet is to express in different ways what has already been said; the poet is not a true creator but rather a "repeater" and "reiterator." True "originality" simply does not exist. Nonetheless, the constant repetition has its own justification. In his prologue to *Obra poética 1923–1964* Borges repeats this concept:

> La literatura impone su magia por artificios; el lector acaba por reconocerlos y desdeñarlos; de ahí la constante necesidad de mínimas o máximas variaciones, que pueden recuperar un pasado o prefigurar un porvenir.[11]

Each generation feels the necessity of repeating what has already been said in its own special way. But, whether recapturing the past or glimpsing at the future, poetry reduces all time to the eternal present of essential "sameness."

Borges uses the poem's final quatrain to sum up the repetitive nature of both art and men's lives. Poetry is like the endlessly flowing river that simultaneously passes and remains fixed; poetry and men are also simultaneously the same and "other." Poetry is "the same" in that it represents the revelation of essences and eternal truths; it is different or "other" because each generation uses its own method or style: the substance is the same, only the packaging is different. Borges, like Heraclitus, maintains that constant change is the very substance of poetry; but paradoxically, by constantly changing, poetry, like the flowing river, remains eternally the same.

In summary, the poem "Arte poética" is a valuable text that concisely presents the essential points that make up Borges' poetics. The poet aspires neither to invent nor to surprise; he contents himself with developing his own unique manner of combining disparate pre-existing elements—themes, feelings, images—into a coherent fabric that communicates profound metaphysical truths.

A few brief words on Borges' literary style are in order. Jaime Alazraki calls Borges' style a willful "anti-style" and quotes Borges himself as stating in *El idioma de los argentinos*: "Plena eficiencia y plena invisibilidad serían las dos perfecciones de cualquier estilo."[12] Borges believes that style should be as simple and unobtrusive as possible, but that it should contribute to creating the overall effect in its own secret way. The tone of Borges' style can be described as "conversational" and "low key." Alazraki summarizes:

> Lo cual probaría que ese estilo invisible por el cual aboga Borges es la resultante de infatigables búsquedas, de alertas vigilancias y de una voluntad literaria que ve la tarea del estilo no como fin en sí mismo, sino como eficaz conductor—de mímima fricción o de resistencia cero—de los temas que ocupan al escritor. (JA p. 154)

Alazraki also provides one of the reasons why Borges constantly revises his texts:

> Los cambios verificados están motivados por un rigoroso afán de precisión, economía y adecuación expresivas: en este acto de fidelidad a los propósitos del tema, el estilo desaparece como entidad en sí misma para convertirse en órgano en función y el concepto de "invisibilidad del estilo" se resume en esa sujeción de la forma a los fines del tema. (JA p. 226)

Using Roland Barthes' terminology, Borges' style can be described as "zero degree writing." Miguel Enguídanos sums up some of the artifices of this "simple" style: "The brilliant insinuation, the mysterious or ironic reference, the small poetic incision, are Borges' chosen expressive means."[13] Borges comments on what his style is supposed to accomplish for him in the prologue to his *Personal Anthology*:

> Croce held that art is expression; to this exigency, or to a deformation of this exigency, we owe the worst literature of our time. . . . Sometimes, I, too, sought expression. I know now that my gods grant me no more than allusion or mention.[14]

Borges repeats this same intuition in "Una rosa amarilla" from *El hacedor*: ". . . podemos mencionar o aludir pero no expresar . . ."[15] Thus, Borges' stylistic goal can be stated as a paradox: to achieve a richly complex simplicity.

Notes

[1] Carlos Bousoño, *Teoría de la expresión poética* (fifth edition; Madrid: Editorial Gredos), vol. I, p. 19–20. Hereafter cited in text as CB.

[2] Jorge Luis Borges, *Obra poética 1923–1964* (Buenos Aires: Emecé Editores, S.A., 1964), p. 11.

[3] Robert Scholes, *Structuralism in Literature* (New Haven: Yale University Press, 1975), p. 29. Hereafter cited in text as RS.

[4] Zunilda Gertel, *Borges y su retorno a la poesía.* (New York: The University of Iowa and Las Américas Publishing Co., 1969), p. 9. Hereafter cited in text as ZG.

[5] Allen W. Phillips, "Borges y su concepto de la metáfora," *Movimientos literarios de vanguardia en iberoamérica* (Mexico, 1965), p. 44. Hereafter cited in text as AP.

[6] Jorge Luis Borges, *Otras inquisiciones* (Buenos Aires: Emecé Editores, 1960), p. 71.

[7] Jorge Luis Borges, *Obras completas* (Buenos Aires: Emecé Editores, 1974), p. 384.

[8] Jean de Milleret, *Entrevistas con Jorge Luis Borges* (Caracas: Monte Avila Editores, 1970), p. 79–80.

[9] Guillermo Sucre, *Borges el poeta* (Caracas: Monte Avila Editores, 1967), p. 36.

[10] *Obra poética 1923–1964*, p. 223–224.

[11] *Obra poética 1923–1964*, p. 11.

[12] Jaime Alazraki, *La prosa narrativa de Jorge Luis Borges* (Madrid: Editorial Gredos, 1968), p. 135. Hereafter cited in text as JA.

[13] Miguel Enguídanos, "Introduction," *Dreamtigers*, Jorge Luis Borges (Austin: University of Texas Press, 1964), p. 14.

[14] Jorge Luis Borges, *A personal anthology*, ed. Anthony Kerrigan (New York: Grove Press, 1967), p. x.

[15] Jorge Luis Borges, *El hacedor* (Buenos Aires: Emecé Editores, 1960), p. 31.

2

Prelude to Fervor

Borges' life is often ignored by literary critics who find it dull and uneventful. Borges himself confesses: "If I were to name the chief event in my life, I should say my father's library. In fact, sometimes I think I have never strayed outside that library."[1] Although Borges' principal life task has been reading and writing, a great deal can be learned from a selective study of key events in the author's life that helped to shape his literary career. Indeed, for a writer so often accused of being cold, intellectual, and removed from the world of daily experience, his work—especially his poetry—is remarkably autobiographical, teeming with references to his own life and that of his family.

Jorge Guillermo and Leonor, Borges' parents, both had an illustrious family pantheon of heroes, many of whom would serve as poetic material for Jorge Luis decades later. For example, the poem "Isidoro Acevedo" commemorates Borges' maternal grandfather, who fought against the dictator Rosas in the nineteenth century; Borges' actual memories of the man are vague since his grandfather died in 1905 while Jorge Luis was still a small child. In a similar manner Borges dedicated his "Conjectural Poem" to Francisco Narciso de Laprida, who after serving at the Tucumán Congress in 1816 (which declared Argentine independence) died in a subsequent civil war. "A Page to Commemorate Colonel Suárez, Victor at Junín" celebrates Borges' mother's maternal grandfather. Francisco Borges (Borges' paternal grandfather) died in one of the Argentine civil wars at age forty-one shortly after marrying Fanny Haslam (Borges' English grandmother), and thus also entered Jorge

Luis' pantheon of military men of action whose exploits were to be later converted into literature.[2]

Jorge Luis Borges' life began August 24, 1899 at his maternal grandparents' one-story house on Tucumán St. near downtown Buenos Aires. Borges tells us that he has no actual memories of this place because his family soon moved to a two-story house in the north-side neighborhood called Palermo. It was a shabby section of town with mainly one-story houses and vacant lots with a large immigrant population including many poor Italians and Spaniards. These immigrant groups were often talked of disparagingly at the Borges' household since they held menial jobs, lacked Argentine roots, and had little culture. Jorge Luis describes his childhood neighborhood in "An Autobiographical Essay" as follows:

> We lived in one of the few two-story homes on our street; the rest of the neighborhood was made up of low houses and vacant lots. I have often spoken of this area as a slum, but I do not quite mean that in the American sense of the word. In Palermo lived shabby, genteel people as well as more undesirable sorts. There was also a Palermo of hoodlums, called *compadritos*, famed for their knife fights, but this Palermo was only later to capture my imagination, since we did our best—our successful best—to ignore it. (AE p. 204)

Borges lived his early years literally cloistered in the confines of the Palermo house and its garden with his parents, maternal grandparents, paternal grandmother (Fanny Haslam), and his sister Norah (born in 1901, and thus two years younger than Jorge Luis). The stifling atmosphere fostered chiefly by Borges' mother's side of the family is described well by Rodríguez Monegal in his literary biography of Borges:

> Borges' family piety reflects his mother's attitude toward her ancestors. Georgie was born and brought up in a house that was, up to a point, a family museum, presided over by the almost ghostly presence of grandfather Acevedo. The place of honor went to the swords that had liberated South America at Junín and Cepeda; the uniforms were carefully preserved against injury from moths; the daguerreotypes framed in black velvet memorialized a parade of dark, sad gentlemen or reserved ladies, many of them prematurely widowed. Georgie was

surrounded by the sacred objects of family history and the ritual repetition of the deeds of his heroic ancestors. These stories of courage and silent dignity in defeat, of poverty and pride, were a permanent part of his heritage. (RM p. 6)

This fascination with the family's military past has haunted Borges all through his life and shows up continually in his work; Borges tells us with typical irony: "So on both sides of my family, I have military forebears; this may account for my yearning after that epic destiny which my gods denied me, no doubt wisely" (AE p. 208).

Later in life Borges criticized the limited vision of the world held by his mother's side of the family which had helped to create some of that stifling atmosphere in his childhood home; in an interview with De Milleret he confides:

> The Acevedos are incredibly ignorant. For instance, for them, descendents of the old Spanish settlers, to be a Protestant is synonymous with being a Jew, that is, an atheist, or a freethinker, or a heretic; in short, they put everything in the same bag. (RM p. 10)

However, it should be noted here that Borges uses only kind words to describe his mother: "I think I inherited from my mother her quality of thinking the best of people and also her strong sense of friendship" (AE p. 207).

Borges' more formal education came from his father and his English grandmother—so much so that Borges learned to read English before he learned to read in Spanish. Thus, English became Borges' language of culture—a strange phenomenon in Argentina at the turn of the century where French was the preferred cultural language. Borges did not attend school until age nine (supposedly to prevent him from contracting childhood diseases, but more probably because his freethinker father did not totally approve of the state schools' curriculum which was laced with strong doses of the Catholic religion and Argentine nationalism. Instead, Borges' father hired an English governess (Miss Tink) to help with Jorge Luis' schooling (RM p. 16–18). Borges' father had a frustrated literary vocation; he wound up being a lawyer who only dabbled in writing, and strongly encouraged his son to fulfill his own unrealized literary destiny. Jorge Guillermo's literary interest was not new to the family history: his father's grandfather, his great-uncle, and a cousin also had had literary leanings. By age six Jorge Luis was saying that he wanted to become a writer, and was attempting imitations of classical Spanish writers. By age nine his translation of Oscar Wilde's "The Little Prince" appeared in *El País*, a Buenos Aires newspaper (AE p. 210–211). Borges credits his father with revealing to him the power of poetry: "the fact that words are not only a means of communication but also magic symbols and music" (AE p. 206–211). Borges also learned powerful lessons of "marginality" from his father who divorced himself from the old Argentine establishment that he considered to be full of racism and snobbery, corrupted by a value system rooted in social inequality and privilege. Jorge Luis learned this lesson so well that he proclaimed to his father that when he grew up he wanted to be a "raté"—a failure when measured with society's traditional yardsticks (RM p. 94). Another trait learned from his father was his lifelong personal modesty: "My father was such a modest man that he would have liked being invisible" (AE p. 206). Rodríguez Monegal tells us that Jorge Guillermo "taught Georgie to shun prizes and despise honors" (RM p. 94). This tendency became so exaggerated in the young Jorge Luis that his lack of self esteem dropped to the point that he was ashamed to accept birthday presents because he deemed himself unworthy of them. His physical frailness and lack of aptitude for a heroic military career like those of so many of his ancestors added to his sense of personal inadequacy:

> Throughout my boyhood, I thought that to be loved would have amounted to an injustice. I did not feel I deserved any particular love, and I remember my birthdays filled me with shame, because everyone heaped gifts on me when I thought that I had done nothing to deserve them—that I was a kind of fake. (AE p. 208–209)

This tendency towards extreme timidity and self-effacement

is a constant in all of Borges' life. In a lighter vein, Borges humorously gives us a glimpse of some of his father's free-thinking anarchist ideas:

> Once, he told me that I should take a good look at soldiers, uniforms, barracks, flags, churches, priests, and butcher shops, since all these things were about to disappear, and I could tell my children that I had actually seen them. The prophecy has not yet come true, unfortunately. (AE p. 206)

However, Guillermo Juan's most important contribution was to encourage his son to be a free, questionning, independent thinker.

We now have a picture of a bookish little boy, who would stammer when excited, without friends his own age, who acted out some of his book-learned fantasies in his childhood games either alone or with his sister Norah—his only playmate—while being a virtual prisoner in his Palermo house and garden. Jorge Luis' childhood terrors included a fear of masks, mirrors, and the noise the old mill out in the yard made during storms. Also surfacing was some unconfortableness upon learning some of the mysteries of sexual expression (RM p. 29–36). These childhood phobias show up as motifs in Borges' writing; for example, the windmill at the Palermo house shows up in the poetry of *Cuaderno San Martín*, there is a poem entitled "The Mirror," and Rodríguez Monegal cites the story of "Emma Zunz" as one example of Borges' negative attitude towards sex in general (RM p. 34–35). The monotony of this routine was broken by trips to the zoo, visits by father's friends, and summer holidays. At the zoo Jorge Luis was fascinated by wild beasts, especially the Indian tiger—the tiger image was to become a lifelong obsession for Borges. As recently as 1972 Borges entitled a book of poetry and its theme poem *El oro de los tigres*. Borges' tigers often symbolize primeval innocence or evil, the exercise of power in the form of gratuitous violence, sexual impulses, or the devouring effects of time—all of which have a clear esthetic appeal for Borges (RM p. 37–40). The visits of Jorge Guillermo's friends were also important diversions for the young Jorge Luis. Two of them—Alvaro Melián Lafinur and Evaristo Carriego—are particularly noteworthy. Alvaro Melián Lafinur was the previously-mentioned cousin with literary leanings; he was admitted into the Argentine Academy of Letters in 1936. Borges tells us that he was a bit of a rogue and that he told him many ribald stories when he was a child; he served as one of the first literary role models for Jorge Luis. Rodríguez Monegal sums up his influence:

> In Georgie's imagination, Alvaro, with his guitar and his aura of being a ladies' man, must have been a tantalizing figure. To the child who lived in a house with a garden from which evil was excluded, Alvaro's visits introduced a bit of the sounds and shapes of the sinful outside world. (RM p. 90)

The other visitor—Evaristo Carriego—was a Palermo neighbor, and a poet with some fame at the time, although he published only a single volume of poetry. He used the poor people of the immigrant neighborhood as his poetic material, expressing their joys, sorrows, and travail. Borges later wrote a biography of him; he tells us in his autobiographical essay:

> Carriego was the man who discovered the literary possibilities of the run-down and ragged outskirts of the city—the Palermo of my boyhood. . . . In 1912, at the age of twenty-nine, he died of tuberculosis, leaving behind a single volume of his work. I remember that a copy of it, inscribed to my father, was one of several Argentine books we had taken to Geneva and that I read and reread there. (AE p. 233–234)

Summer holidays were the third activity that represented a break in Borges' childhood routine. Some of these were spent in Uruguay (at Paso Molino, then on the outskirts of Montevideo) at the villa of the Haedo family—cousins of Leonor (Borges' mother). They also had a ranch to the west on the Uruguay River; Borges is still proud to speak of his swimming in the swift river waters. In *Luna de enfrente* (1925) Borges writes of his pleasant memories of Uruguay—a fusion of happy memories from both sides of the River Plate. At about age ten, while visiting some other relatives northwest of

Buenos Aires near San Nicolás, he discovered for the first time the "endless distance" of the pampa and saw real gauchos who he found glamorous since he had already read about them in books (AE p. 212–213). Other summers were spent in the small town of Adrogué, located just south of Buenos Aires; at first the Borges family rented a house there, but later just stayed at the Hotel Las Delicias. Borges explains:

> Adrogué then was a lost and undisturbed maze of summer homes surrounded by iron fences with masonry planters on the gate posts, of parks, of streets that radiated out of the many plazas, and of the ubiquitous smell of eucalyptus trees. We continued to visit Adrogué for decades. (AE p. 212)

The sentimental attachment Borges had for Adrogué is documented by Alicia Jurado who decades later accompanied Borges there on a special pilgrimage:

> I went with him to say good-by to the Adrogué Hotel before it was demolished; we walked in darkness through ravaged floors, glimpsing patios and windows which brought memories to him, sitting on the broken bench of a ruined garden he loved and in a square full of trees and covered with fallen leaves from which he pointed out to me the house they had had for many a summer. (RM p. 64)

In 1977 Borges published a book of poems entitled *Adrogué* containing essentially a selection of previously published works; in the preface, after stating flatly that his favorite cities are Buenos Aires, Adrogué, Geneva, and Austin, he rambles on at length about Adrogué's importance in his life:

> En cualquier parte del mundo en que me encuentre, cuando siento el olor de los eucaliptus, estoy en Adrogué. Adrogué era eso: un largo laberinto tranquilo de calles arboladas, de verjas y de quintas; un laberinto de vastas noches quietas que mis padres gustaban recorrer. Quintas en las que uno adivinaba la vida detrás de las quintas. De algún modo siempre estuve aquí, siempre estoy aquí. Los lugares se llevan, los lugares están en uno. Sigo entre los eucaliptus y en el laberinto, el lugar en que uno puede perderse. Supongo que uno también puede perderse en el paraíso.[3]

The motifs of night, shadow, dreams, nightmares, mirrors, and labyrinths that are so common in Borges' writing can be traced back to these childhood summer memories. Borges affirms this view:

> Muchos argumentos, muchas escenas, muchos poemas que he imaginado nacieron de Adrogué o se sitúan en ella. Siempre que hablo de jardines, siempre que hablo de árboles estoy en Adrogué, he pensado en esta ciudad, no es necesario que la nombre.[4]

Back in Buenos Aires, at age nine, Borges was finally sent to a state school to continue his education; he despised that experience: "As I wore spectacles and dressed in an Eton collar and tie, I was jeered at and bullied by most of my schoolmates, who were amateur hooligans" (AE p. 212). Jorge Luis had almost no school friends and suffered through this phase of his education; in reality, his father continued to be his principal teacher.

Jorge Guillermo was forced into early retirement from the law profession due to his failing eyesight—a malady that would later afflict Jorge Luis. In ten days (in summer 1914) he packed up the family and left for Europe. Borges recounts:

> The idea of the trip was for my sister and me to go to school in Geneva; we were to live with my maternal grandmother, who traveled with us and eventually died there, while my parents toured the Continent. (AE p. 214)

After they all made short visits to England and then to Paris, plans went awry; the children started school in Geneva (fall 1914) but the outbreak of World War I forced Borges' parents to seek refuge in Geneva and abort their European tour. Later Fanny Haslam braved German submarines to join the rest of the Borges clan in Geneva, thus reconstituting the entire family circle—now in Swiss exile—that Jorge Luis had enjoyed at the Palermo home. Although he expressed dislike for the damp, drizzly climate, Borges' education and social life progressed well at the Collège Calvin where he studied and eventually completed his secondary education; he was popular and made valuable adolescent friendships—friends with whom he could discuss literature and philosophy in an intelligent fashion. He learned French and Latin and studied French literature, reading realist and naturalist novels (which he later claimed to have disliked), and symbolist poetry (which he found to be more amenable). Borges' symbolist poetry readings included Verlaine, Rimbaud, and Mallarmé. Speaking of Mallarmé's importance, Rodríguez Monegal states: "His persona (the poet who is totally dedicated to writing and to whom the world makes sense only in a book) influenced Borges' own concept of literature and of the literary mind" (RM p. 122). His non-school readings continued to be mainly in English. He was fascinated with Carlyle's *Sartor Resartus* (a parody of German romantic philosophy; it reviews and summarizes a nonexistent book—a technique Borges would later emulate). From Carlyle (whom Borges later dismissed for his political views) Borges gleaned the idea that the world is "unreal like a nightmare and atrocious" (RM p. 130). Borges also developed a passion for Gilbert Keith Chesterton's stories—from which Jorge Luis began to develop his concept of the detective story and his feeling for dealing with evil. Another English writer Borges discovered during this period was DeQuincey; the two share an interest in "strange heresies, secret societies, philosophical or religious problems (suicide is one of the most noticeable), odd linguistic theories, murder and violent death" (RM p. 127). Memory, dreams, insomnia, and analogical relationships can be added to this list of mutual interests.

One of Borges' outside interests during his Swiss sojourn was to learn German as a key to German philosophy. After trying to learn German with limited success by using Kant's *Critique of Pure Reason* as a primer, Borges switched to Heine's *Lyrical Intermezzo* and made fine progress. He soon read Meyrink's *Der Golem* (published in 1915); it is full of theosophy and the occult—a rabbi creates a creature out of mud to be his servant. Borges' story "The Circular Ruins" was clearly influenced by this work; he also has a poem called "The Golem." Borges continued his German odyssey with the philosophical papers of Fritz Mauthner; in a 1962 interview with James Irby, Borges speaks favorably of Mauthner:

> He believed language only serves either to hide reality or for esthetic expression. His dictionary of philosophy, one of the books I have consulted with great pleasure, is really a collection of essays on different subjects, such as the soul, the world, the spirit, the conscience, *etc.* (RM p. 138)

One of Borges' most important discoveries was Schopenhauer:

> At some point while in Switzerland, I began reading Schopenhauer. Today, were I to choose a single philosopher, I would choose him. If the riddle of the universe can be stated in words, I think these words would be in his writings. (AE p. 216–217)

Some of Schopenhauer's most appealing ideas for Borges include the premise that art is the only way to meaning and that it can create "a meaningful natural cosmos out of the crumbling social order," and the idea of the denial of the existence of time and the subsequent erosion of both external reality and individual personality (RM p. 139–140). In his essay "The Nothingness of Personality" (appearing in *Inquisiciones*, 1925) Borges quotes Schopenhauer as saying: "everyone who said I during all that time before I was born, was truly I" (RM p. 140). Borges makes the point that the ego is not "individual" but a mere "logical urgency." His readings of Nietzsche also centered on the theme of the denial of the existence of time and on the theory of the eternal return. On his nineteenth birthday in 1918, Borges asked for and received a German encyclopedia to continue his studies of German philosophy and literature; it is also of interest to note the beginnings of Borges' fascination with encyclopedias as basic sources of knowledge that attempt to encompass all human wisdom within the confines of a single work—the encyclopedia strives to be *the book*.

When Borges' maternal grandmother died in 1918 the family left Geneva—where Borges had completed his secondary education—and moved to Lugano. In the absence of his intellectual group of friends, he grew closer to his sister Norah; the two spent long hours rowing on the lake and reciting French symbolist poetry. His experience with German literature deepened with his discovery of the German expressionist poets; his readings included poets such as Johannes Beccher, Wilhelm Klemm, Ernst Stadler, and August Stramm. Borges gave the following definition of the group in *Inquisiciones*: "Vehemence in the attitudes, and in the depth of their poetry, abundance of images and the postulation of universal brotherhood: that was expressionism" (RM p. 146).

Borges judged the other "-isms" that were then flourishing to be frivolous, lacking the seriousness of purpose and depth of feeling so evident in the expressionists. Borges tells us:

> I became, however, very interested in German expressionism and still think of it as beyond other contemporary schools, such as imagism, cubism, futurism, surrealism and so on. (AE p. 216)

At this point in his life Borges shared many common interests with the expressionists: magic, dreams, Eastern religions and philosophy, the idea of world brotherhood, the coining of words, the erotic, the political, and the use of violent, dazzling images. Rodríguez Monegal sums up the effect of these poets on Borges' literary career:

> In his readings he had come across a group of young poets who wrote violently about love and war, about despair and hope, about a world brotherhood. They were called "expressionists" and were related to the avant-garde poets, called cubists or futurists, dadaists or imagists, who since the beginning of the century had one thing in common: the need to radically change the literary and artistic establishment's concept of art and of the world. The expressionists were the first truly modern poets Georgie read, the ones who introduced him to the new poetics. They achieved what neither Father with his nineteenth-century taste nor his closest Swiss friends with their fondness for symbolism could do: they made him truly conversant with what was revolutionary in contemporary letters. (RM p. 144)

Through his study of the expressionists, Borges stumbled

upon Whitman; it was the beginning of a lifelong love affair. Borges confides that:

> For a time, I thought of Whitman not only as a great poet but as the only poet. In fact, I thought that all poets the world over had been merely leading up to Whitman until 1855, and that not to imitate him was a proof of ignorance. (AE p. 217)

In *Inquisiciones* Borges explains his attraction to Whitman in more concrete terms: "We can also see in Whitman the whole business of living; in Whitman also breathes the miraculous gratitude for the concrete and tactile and many-colored ways things are" (RM p. 149). However, what most attracted Borges to Whitman was the denial of the individual personality—the "I"—to express the soul of the entire universe; Whitman's poetry represented the culmination and logical summation of his readings of German philosophy and the expressionist poets.

Borges began writing poems during this period in Switzerland. He explains:

> I had been writing sonnets in English and in French. The English sonnets were poor imitations of Wordsworth, and the French, in their own watery way, were imitative of symbolist poetry. . . . I knew, however, that Spanish would be my unavoidable destiny. (AE p. 218)

None of these earliest works is known to exist; however, a group of Borges' expressionist-influenced poems written in Spanish has been preserved.

The Borgeses decided to spend some time in Spain before returning to Buenos Aires:

> We decided to go home, but to spend a year or so in Spain first. Spain at that time was slowly being discovered by Argentines. . . . In Buenos Aires, Spaniards always held menial jobs—as domestic servants, waiters, and laborers—or were small tradesmen, and we Argentines never thought of ourselves as Spanish. We had, in fact, left off being Spaniards in 1816, when we declared our independence from Spain. (AE p. 218)

Borges clearly does not try to cover up his general lack of esteem for Spaniards and things Spanish. After arriving in Barcelona by train, the Borgeses sailed to Palma de Mallorca and later took up residence in the small town of Valldemosa. Borges deromanticizes the trip: "We went to Majorca because it was cheap, beautiful, and had hardly any tourists but ourselves" (AE p. 219). It is clear that Borges, armed with Whitman and the newest European literary trends, viewed Spain as culturally backward, and not as a place to rediscover his cultural roots and to find new literary stimulation. In Mallorca Borges studied Latin (and Virgil) with a priest; Borges' knowledge of Latin helped him develop his excellent command of syntax, his uncanny feeling for words, and the ability to use words in their etymological sense rather than their conventional one. Borges' other activities in Mallorca included giving his father some startling expressionist metaphors for his novel *El caudillo* (that otherwise has a more nineteenth-century tone), and in his autobiographical essay he touts his swimming ability—about the only way to fulfill in reality his esthetic fantasy of being a man of action. During this time, Borges was also busy writing essays on esthetics. One of his Geneva classmates helped him to get an article published there in *La Feuille* (August 20, 1919); it is a review of recently published essays of Pío Baroja and Azorín. In it Borges flatly states that "all the intelligent Spaniards will tell you that their country is not worth anything now" (RM p. 155). In addition, Borges' youthful interest in anti-establishment politics, in the peace movement, and utopian visions of society evidence themselves.

Next the Borgeses moved on to Seville to spend the winter (1919); Borges shows contempt for the literary atmosphere he found there:

> In Seville, I fell in with the literary group formed around *Grecia*. This group, who called themselves ultraists, had set out to renew literature, a branch of the arts of which they knew nothing whatever. (AE p. 220)

He goes on to poke fun at *Grecia*'s editor Isaac del Vando

35

Villar who Borges claims had his work written for him by his assistants rather than being bothered by writing something himself. However, the importance of the Seville experience was to put Borges in direct contact with actual writers and let him participate in Spanish literary life (which Borges now sees in a more positive light). In a 1962 interview with Irby, Borges sums up this positive aspect of Spanish literary life:

> I didn't discover anything special except a generous style of oral life; that atmosphere so lively and genuine, of literary gatherings and cafés, in which literature was alive in a very striking way: an atmosphere which . . . had never existed in Argentina. In Geneva . . . there was no literary life, although I had there many literary friends of different nationalities, and there were excellent bookstores where one could find the best of the current literature. (RM p. 157–158)

This "pressing of the literary flesh" was one of the most direct benefits Borges derived from his stay in Spain.

Borges describes an event in Seville that is a landmark in his burgeoning career:

> The winter of 1919–1920 we spent in Seville, where I saw my first poem into print. It was titled "Hymn to the Sea" and appeared in the magazine *Grecia*, in its issue of December 31, 1919. In the poem, I tried my hardest to be Walt Whitman:
>
>> O sea! O myth! O sun! O wide resting place!
>> I know why I love you. I know that we are both very old,
>> that we have known each other for centuries . . .
>> O Protean, I have been born of you—
>> both of us chained and wandering,
>> both of us hungering for stars,
>> both of us with hopes and disappointments . . . !
>
> Today, I hardly think of the sea, or even of myself, as hungering for stars. Years after, when I came across Arnold Bennett's phrase "the third-rate grandiose," I understood at once what he meant. And yet when I arrived in Madrid a few months later, as this was the only poem I had ever printed, people there thought of me as a singer of the sea.[5]

This first published poem is characterized by long lines, unusual length (over sixty lines), and a hodgepodge of influences—not only Whitman, but also the French symbolists and a strong dose of German expressionism with its violent imagery. Some examples of this startling imagery include waves that "shout" and "pant" ("las olas que gritan" and "olas jadeantes"), steel waters ("aguas de acero"), the repetition of the adjective "bloody" ("sangrienta"), and a vision of the sun burning in the waters like a red flag ("cuando el sol en sus aguas cual bandera escarlata flamea"). "Himno del mar" is also of interest because it undoubtedly contains the greatest concentration of erotic imagery found anywhere in Borges' poetry. Borges speaks of the sea as "athletic" and "naked" ("atlético y desnudo") and after plunging into the waters, his body stretched like a bow, struggles with the sea's swift muscles ("mi cuerpo tendido como un arco lucha contra tus músculos raudos"). Speaking of his journey to reach the sea, Borges compares the long trip to a kiss: "El camino fue largo como un beso." The repeated sexual imagery is clearly the principal vehicle used to forge the unity the poem seeks to create between the poet and the universe, symbolized by the sea. The eroticism reaches its zenith in lines such as these:

> Del mar cuando besa los pechos dorados de
> / vírgenes playas que aguardan sedientas;
> * * *
> Y en la sagrada media noche yo he tejido
> / guirnaldas
> De besos sobre carnes y labios que se
> / ofrendaban,[6]

The poet then renounces sexual relations with mere mortals for a permanent union with the sea. However, the theme of the poem—the negation of the individual personality of the poet by means of a total, harmonious fusion (and joyous reunion) with the natural forces of the universe—despite its declamatory first person tone, is clearly in the mainstream of Borges' thought. In its totality "Hymn to the Sea" is a unique poem; there is truly virtually nothing comparable to it in the rest of Borges' work.

From Seville the Borgeses moved on to Madrid where Jorge Luis became friends with Rafael Cansinos-Asséns, one of the foremost literary vanguard figures at that time (considered by many to be the head of the ultraist group if not actually the inventor of the term "ultraísmo"). Borges joined Cansinos-Asséns' literary circle at the Café Colonial in Madrid where literature, the arts, and esthetics were discussed from midnight to daybreak. Borges describes the scene:

> Cansinos would propose a subject—The Metaphor, Free Verse, The Traditional Forms of Poetry, Narrative Poetry, The Adjective, The Verb. In his own quiet way, he was a dictator, allowing no unfriendly allusions to contemporary writers and trying to keep the talk on a high plane. (AE p. 221–222)

The group frowned on local color and wanted to be European rather than merely Spanish. What Borges most admired in Cansinos-Asséns was the fact that he was a knowledgeable sincere man of letters who lived for literature rather than fame or money. Although Borges would later label himself as a disciple of Cansinos-Asséns, he concedes in his autobiographical essay that the true degree of influence Cansinos exercised on him was not all that large: "What I got from him, chiefly, was the pleasure of literary conversation. Also, I was stimulated by him to far-flung reading" (AE p. 222).

Cansinos-Asséns also drew attention to the creationist theories and poetry of Huidobro which Borges found less attractive because he deemed them to be too playful and lacking a serious foundation. It was during this period that Borges rediscovered Spanish literature; the authors he then preferred included Quevedo, Cervantes, Unamuno, and Baroja.

Borges visited Ramón Gómez de la Serna's rival literary group which met at the Pombo—a small, smoke-filled Madrid bar; the more frivolous atmosphere disgusted Borges: "I went there once, and didn't like the way they behaved" (AE p. 223). Ramón Gómez de la Serna helped introduce the vanguard movements into Spain by writing in Madrid magazines about movements such as futurism as early as 1909. His greguerías composed of humor plus metaphor were his way of reaching his proclaimed goal of "fumigating" nature with new images—all of which coincide with the key goals of the ultraists (RM p. 162). Ramón Gómez de la Serna cannot be seen as a true rival of Cansinos' ultraist group, but rather as another aspect of it.

The ultraist movement itself was chiefly the brain child of Cansinos-Asséns, who wrote its first real manifesto in the fall of 1918, signing the names of about eight other men to it instead of his own; it proclaimed the necessity of an "ultraism" (a more precise philosophical base was clearly lacking):

> Nuestra literatura debe renovarse, debe lograr su *ultra*, como hoy pretende lograrlo nuestro pensamiento científico y político. Nuestro lema será *ultra*, y en nuestro credo cabrán todas las tendencias sin distinción. Más tarde estas tendencias lograrán su núcleo y su definición. Por el momento creemos suficiente lanzar este grito de renovación y anunciar la publicación de una revista que llevará este título: *Ultra*, y en la que sólo lo nuevo hallará acogida.[7]

Borges' main role in the ultraist movement was to provide the theoretical base for the movement by publishing essays or manifestos on ultraism. One of the early ones appeared in *Grecia* (January 31, 1920); entitled "On the Margins of Modern Lyrics," it postulates that ultraist poetry should express a new spirit and a new point of view: "the fertile premise which considers words not as bridges to ideas but as ends in themselves finds in ultraism its culmination" (RM p. 164). In "Anatomy of My Ultra" (*Grecia*, May 20, 1921) Borges affirms an interest in sensation itself rather than a mere description of the spatial or temporal setting; ultraism is the art of transferring naked emotion to the reader, free from metaphysical, egocentric, or ironic baggage and superfluous information. A similar article in *Cosmópolis* (Madrid, November 1921) again focuses on the importance of the metaphor and rhythm in the poetic process. The rhythm Borges refers to here is not meter but rather a rhythm that is "liberated" by metaphors (RM p. 164). Borges was also the principal diffusor of the German expressionist poets, who were not well known in Spain, publishing in

Spanish literary magazines both translations of the actual poems and essays about expressionist theories.

Guillermo de Torre—who believed himself to be one of the movement's principal theorists along with Borges—summarizes the key ultraist dogmas:

> ... reintegración lírica e introducción de una nueva temática. Para conseguir lo primero utilizó, sobrevaloró la imagen y la metáfora, suprimiendo la anécdota, lo narrativo, la efusión retórica. Para lo segundo se proscribió lo sentimental, sólo aceptado en su envés irónico, impura y deliberadamente mezclado al mundo moderno, visto éste nunca de un modo directo, sino en un cruce de sensaciones. Se rompía así con la continuidad del discurso lógico, dando relieve contrariamente a las percepciones fragmentarias, y entendiendo con ello mantener la pureza del flujo lírico. Un afán tan ingenuo como heroico nos dominaba: "La miel de la añoranza—escribía Jorge Luis Borges—no nos deleita y quisiéramos ver todas las cosas en una primicial floración." (DT p. 61)

After this purification process what was left was the image, not simple, direct or a reproduction of reality, but rather an indirect one bearing multiple levels of meaning (DT p. 63). De Torre also lists Borges' own summary of the four essential points of ultraism:

1. Reducción de la lírica a su elemento primordial: la metáfora.
2. Tachadura de las frases medianeras, los nexos, y los adjetivos inútiles.
3. Abolición de los trebejos ornamentales, el confesionalismo, la circunstanciación, las prédicas y la nebulosidad rebuscada.
4. Síntesis de dos o más imágenes en una que ensanche de ese modo su facultad de sugerencia. (DT p. 64)

Then Borges further distills these theories: "Los poemas ultraicos constan, pues, de una serie de metáforas, cada una de las cuales tiene sugestividad propia y compendia una visión inédita de algún fragmento de vida" (DT p. 64). Some of the magazines that trumpeted the new esthetics included *Grecia*, *Cervantes*, *Ultra*, *Tableros*, and *Horizonte* (DT p. 67–74). In *Reflector* (which had a single issue in December 1920), Borges wrote an article on De Torre's "Manifiesto Vertical"; this tract showed an un-ultraist willingness among the ultraists to be more eclectic—in other words, the movement was disintegrating (DT p. 73–74). The game-like nature of much of ultraism's theories are clearly in evidence in these magazines; a few quotes on ultraism from *Ultra* communicate the mood of the period:

> Los ultraístas hemos descubierto la cuadratura del círculo.
> El ultraísmo es la rana que crió pelos.
> El ultraísmo consiste en volver el mundo del revés.
> El ultraísmo es el tren que pasa siempre. Hay que subir y bajar en marcha.
> Defendemos una antiliteratura implacable que acabe con todos los tópicos. Ya hemos afirmado que "la literatura no existe: el ultraísmo lo ha matado."
> De ahí el título de nuestra próxima encuesta, dirigida a los jóvenes y viejos profesionales: ¿Por qué escribe usted aún? (DT p. 71)

However, in the final analysis, even Guillermo De Torre was forced to admit the existence of a huge gap between the new esthetic theories and the literary works actually produced: "El ultraísmo fue más pródigo en 'gestos y ademanes' que en obras, más rico en revistas de conjunto que en obras individuales" (DT p. 65). De Torre further accepts this much diminished status of ultraism in the following summation: "Ahora bien, sucede que la importancia del ultraísmo fue quizá mayor en sus continuadores indirectos que en sus iniciadores voluntarios" (DT p. 95). If De Torre had Borges in mind as one of those "indirect offshoots" of ultraism, most contemporary criticism tends to disagree with such a thesis. Guillermo Sucre believes that although Borges defined, defended, and exalted ultraism at this stage of his career, for Borges ultraism was purely theoretical and intellectual, more of a game than a serious endeavor: "Borges fue ultraísta más por sentido del juego, de la aventura, que por convicción estética."[8] Néstor Ibarra states flatly that "Borges dejó de ser ultraísta a partir del primer verso ultraísta que escribió."[9] In an interview with Jean De Milleret, Borges himself repudiates ultraist dogma in the strongest of terms: "Todo aquello era tan ingenuo, y además tan tonto, esa idea de reducir toda la poesía a un solo artificio: la metáfora."[10]

What remains of all this clamor are Borges' poems, published in the magazines of the period. In his autobiographical essay Borges prefers to admit to having published only three or four poems; Rodríguez Monegal estimates the number at about eleven while Carlos Meneses in a study published in 1978 has managed to unearth eighteen. Borges claims to have written a book of literary and political essays, *Los naipes del tahur*, and a book of poetry probably entitled *Psalmos rojos* (under the influence of Cansinos-Asséns' "psalms" in *El candelabro de los siete brazos*). Borges also says that he destroyed both of these unpublished works before leaving Spain. The poems were "in free verse and in praise of the Russian Revolution, the brotherhood of man, and pacifism" (AE p. 223). In general, one would have to agree with Carlos Meneses who maintains that this early poetry more clearly reflects German expressionism than Spanish ultraism (CM p. 15). However, a closer examination of this poetry yields some surprises, and foreshadows Borges' literary trajectory. Only three of these poems deal directly with the Russian Revolution: "Rusia" (*Grecia*, #48, Seville, Sept. 1, 1920), "Gesta Maximalista" (*Ultra*, #3, Madrid, Feb. 20, 1921), and "Guardia Roja" (*Tableros*, #1, Madrid, Nov. 15, 1921).[11] The poem "Guardia Roja" begins with a very ultraist line: "El viento es la bandera que se enreda en las lanzas"; following are more startling images such as "ya grita el sol," and sexual overtones more characteristic of the expressionists. In "Rusia" the violent imagery continues: "el sol crucificado en los ponientes / se pluraliza en la vocinglería / de las torres del Kremlin." Most notable here is the mixing of the sunset with blood imagery, which characterizes the "crepuscular poems" of this period. "Gesta Maximalista" tries to convey the awe of the multitudes at the triumph of the Russian Revolution: "Pájaro rojo vuela un estandarte / sobre la hirsuta muchedumbre estática." The sexual imagery again surges to the forefront when the bayonets of the passing soldiers are called "el candelabro de los mil y un falos." Influence seekers can have their fill with the aforementioned line. The "candelabra" comes from a Cansinos-Asséns book title, the "thousand and one" from the Arabian Nights tales Borges so loved, and the sexual imagery from the German expressionists. Futurism also shows its face in the poem's "cathedral airplane," an image which dominates another poem of this period entitled "Catedral." "Trinchera" (*Grecia*, #43, June 1, 1920) is also a war poem, but related to the horrors of World War I in general as opposed to having a specific relationship with the October Revolution as in the case of the three previously mentioned poems. The bayonets as phallic symbols appear here also; the lines are long and the imagery expressionist:

> El mundo se ha perdido y los ojos de los muertos
> / lo buscan
> El silencio aúlla en los horizontes hundidos.

"Insomnio" (*Grecia*, #49, Madrid, Sept. 15, 1920) is a unique and very autobiographical poem (it is an unusually long poem with long lines) in which Borges describes how he staggered home drunk with a friend after a night of reveling. This documenting of his bohemian literary life in Spain is replete with references to alcohol, drunkenness, and drugs; one terse line sums up the drives that gave birth to this poem: "Ira. Anarquismo. Hambre sexual." The poem is another collage of influences. Futurism appears in the form of a "hangar" used to house emotions. The obsessive relating of blood imagery with the sunset repeats itself: "Me he desangrado en demasiados ponientes." Violent imagery predominates; rain drops become blood and then are called "los dientes de la obscuridad que roen las paredes." Some lines are remarkable for their graphic realism: "Y en el cráneo sigue vibrando esta lamentable llama de / alcohol que no quiere apagarse." In a similar vein Borges describes the lack of equilibrium that characterized his gait and that of his companion: "Al vernos navegar tan espirales se ríen a carcajadas las puertas." In short, the poem gives a clearer vision of the seamier side of Borges' stay in Madrid.

"Poema" (*Baleares*, Palma de Mallorca, Oct. 20, 1920) shows mostly ultraist influence according to Meneses (CM p. 28). Borges mentions the poem's last line—"Cajita negra para el violín que se ha roto"—as having been originally written in French while he was still living in Switzerland; Borges dismisses it as a boyhood exercise (AE p. 218). In "Catedral" (*Baleares*, #131, Feb. 15, 1921) and "Mañana" (*Ultra*, #1, Madrid, Jan. 27, 1921) Borges places considerable importance on the placement of the words on the page; Borges' foray into graphics is very mild when compared to Apollinaire and some of the creationist games. This preoccupation with the physical appearance of the poem on the printed page affects about half of the poems written during this early period in Borges' career. The futurist image of the cathedral as a stone airplane is the most notable feature of "Catedral," while "Mañana" is a celebration of morning with daring imagery, most of it ultraist, but some of it is futurist: the world is "ebrio como una hélice." Futurism is also in evidence in a poem that Meneses overlooks in his collection of Borges' early poems. Entitled "Tranvías" (*Ultra*, Madrid, March 30, 1921), the poem, laden with ultraist imagery, is a eulogy of the streetcar; it can be seen as an example of how man's technological progress can be transformed into poetic material, thus fusing the world of art with that of applied science.[12]

"Aldea" (*Ultra*, #21, Madrid, Jan. 1, 1922), "Prismas" (*Ultra*, #7, Madrid, March 1, 1921), "Singladura" (*Ultra*, #8, Madrid, April 20, 1921), "Ultimo rojo sol" (*Ultra*, #20, Madrid, Dec. 15, 1921), "Montaña" (*Tableros*, #2, Madrid, Dec. 15, 1922), and to a certain extent "Distancia" (*Ultra*, #9, Madrid, April 30, 1921) can all be called crepuscular poems in which the sun's dying rays blur the sharp edges of reality to produce a somber mood and strange visions. In this early series of poems, the sun, moon, wind, musical instruments (for example, the guitar in "Prismas" and the violin in "Distancia"), are often used to express sadness, pessimism or pain. "Aldea" describes the sunset in a small village; despite the poem's seemingly violent beginning—"El poniente de pie como un Arcángel / tiranizó el sendero"—the general tone of the poem is restful. The "Arcángel" metaphor is repeated in "Ultimo rojo sol," the lines "Las esquilas recogen la tristeza / dispersa de las tardes" resurface in "Prismas," and the image of "la luna nueva" compared to "una vocecita bajo el cielo" reappears in "Montaña." Thus, this period shows us a Borges who is working and reworking a limited corpus of material, freely borrowing material from his previous poems in order to create new variations on similar themes. Some of these images carry over almost verbatim into *Fervor de Buenos Aires*; for example, a fragment from "Prismas"—"vamos abriendo como ramas las calles"—appears in the *Fervor de Buenos Aires* poem "Benarés" as "la luz va abriendo como ramas las calles." "Ultimo rojo sol" is probably the most dramatic of the sunset or "twilight" mood poems:

> y un poniente monstruoso
> que tiene abiertas todas sus alas
> (dolorida y desnuda
> una guitarra brusca se desangra)
> El poniente de pie como un Arcángel
> tiraniza la calle

The poem "Montaña" repeats these same motifs, with the shadow of the mountain as the backdrop for the sunset whereas the sea provides the locale for the sunset in "Singladura."

The conclusion to be drawn from these "crepuscular poems"—which constitute about half of Borges' extant poetry from this period—is that the poet's chief preoccupation at this time was the creation and the expression of his own inner reality using vanguard techniques as the building blocks of his poetry. The war, revolutions, pacifism, and universal brotherhood as poetic themes were already clearly losing favor.

The last three of these early Borges poems published in Spain are: "Escaparate" (*Tableros*, #3, Madrid, Jan. 15, 1922), "Sala vacía" and "Siesta" (both published in *Ultra*, #24, Madrid, March 15, 1922). All of these poems clearly have more affinities with *Fervor de Buenos Aires* than with the earlier poems. In "Siesta," the theme is time dammed up by a house's shutters; it is one of the first concrete examples of the dichotomy in Borges' world between "sunny outsides," where reality exists and time flows freely, and "dark interiors" where time slows down or seems to stop. "Sala vacía" is another excellent example of the dark interiors with their heavy, sturdy furniture, daguerreotypes, and mirrors as opposed to the light, clamor, and "vertigo" of the street. The fact that "Sala vacía" appears with the same title but in a revised form in *Fervor de Buenos Aires* is proof that these poems represent a dramatic transition in Borges' production from a preoccupation with the external world's political and social problems to the relative safety of his own inner emotional world consisting largely of his readings and actual life experiences. The poem "Escaparate" foretells with uncanny accurateness the entire unfolding of Borges' life. In the poem, Borges compares himself to the figure of a toy Chinese warrior hero made out of porcelain who is frozen for eternity just out of reach of all the goals he seeks. Life is an eternal, frustrating search for the ultimate, for absolutes which even if found will remain always unattainable:

> Pero siempre el espacio dorado los separa,
> siempre el héroe venera los suyos sin lograr abrazarlos
> Así yo ignoraré mis amores.
> Así yo deberé desconocerte.

By 1922, Borges was aware of his destiny: literature—the protective glass in the showcase window—would shelter him from the terrors and vicissitudes of life but immobilize him like a porcelain figurine just short of being able to touch some of his cherished life goals. As an old man looking back on his life Borges tells us what he is still seeking: "What I'm out for now is peace, the enjoyment of thinking and of friendship, and, though it may be too ambitious, a sense of loving and being loved" (AE p. 260).

Notes

[1] Jorge Luis Borges, "An Autobiographical Essay," *The Aleph and Other Stories 1933–1969*, Norman Thomas di Giovanni, editor and translator (New York: E.P. Dutton, 1978), p. 209. Hereafter cited in text as AE.

[2] Emir Rodríguez Monegal, *Jorge Luis Borges: A Literary Biography* (New York: E.P. Dutton, 1978), p. 3–8. Hereafter cited in text as RM.

[3] Jorge Luis Borges, *Adrogué* (Adrogué, República Argentina: Ediciones Adrogué, 1977), p. 7.

[4] *Adrogué*, p. 7.

[5] "An Autobiographical Essay," p. 220. The complete Spanish text of this poem can be found in Carlos Meneses' book (p. 57–58).

[6] Carlos Meneses, *Poesía juvenil de Jorge Luis Borges* (Barcelona: Editor José J. de Olañeta, 1978), p. 57–58. Hereafter cited in text as CM.

[7] Guillermo de Torre, *Ultraísmo, existencialismo, y objetivismo en literatura* (Madrid: Ediciones Guadarrama, 1968), p. 60. Hereafter cited in text as DT.

[8] Guillermo Sucre, *Borges el poeta* (Caracas: Monte Avila Editores, 1967), p. 36.

[9] Jean de Milleret, *Entrevistas con Jorge Luis Borges* (Caracas: Monte Avila Editores, 1970), p. 34.

[10] De Milleret, p. 34.

[11] Meneses, p. 57–76. The complete texts of most of Borges' early poems can be found in these pages of Meneses' book.

[12] Guillermo de Torre, "Para la prehistoria ultraísta de Borges," *Jorge Luis Borges: El escritor y la crítica*, Jaime Alazraki, editor (Madrid: Taurus Ediciones, 1976), p. 88.

3

Buenos Aires Fervor

In his autobiographical essay, Borges tells us of his return to Buenos Aires in March 1921:

> It came to me as a surprise, after living in so many European cities . . . to find that my native town had grown, and that it was now a very large, sprawling, and almost endless city of low buildings with flat roofs, stretching west toward what geographers and literary hands call the pampa. It was more than a homecoming; it was a rediscovery. I was able to see Buenos Aires keenly and eagerly because I had been away from it for a long time. Had I never gone abroad, I wonder whether I would ever have seen it with the peculiar shock and glow that it now gave me. The city—not the whole city, of course, but a few places in it that became emotionally significant to me—inspired the poems of my first published book, *Fervor de Buenos Aires*.[1]

Borges goes on to tell us that he wrote the poems for *Fervor de Buenos Aires* in 1921 and 1922 and that the book was published in early 1923. On the surface of things Borges seems to have continued in Buenos Aires the same Bohemian life style he had known in Madrid, after settling into a house near his old Palermo neighborhood. Besides walking the streets to rediscover his city, Borges began a busy literary life, becoming the leader of a group of young poets including his cousin Guillermo Juan Borges, Eduardo González Lanuza, Norah Lange, Francisco Piñero, and Roberto Ortelli. Referring to the fact that he is known as the father of Argentine ultraism, Borges explains that:

> . . . we came to the conclusion that Spanish ultraism was overburdened—after the manner of futurism—with modernity and gadgets. We were unimpressed by railway trains, by propellers, by

airplanes, and by electric fans. While in our manifestos we still upheld the primacy of the metaphor and the elimination of transitions and decorative adjectives, what we wanted to write was essential poetry— poems beyond the here and now, free of local color and contemporary circumstances. (AE p. 225–226)

Borges goes on to cite the poem "Llaneza" ("Plainness") from *Fervor de Buenos Aires* as a good example of the type of poetry he now aspired to write. Perhaps the most concise statement Borges made on the nature of Argentine ultraism appeared in a review he wrote of a book of poems by González Lanuza: "Ultraism in Buenos Aires was the ambition to obtain an absolute art which did not depend on the uncertain prestige of words and which lasted in the eternity of language as a conviction of beauty."[2]

Borges and his literary circle decided that they needed a magazine to propagate their ideas; the result was *Prisma* which had only two issues "published" (it was a one-page mural magazine plastered on walls) in December 1921 and March 1922. Borges describes it: "Each issue was a large single sheet and contained a manifesto and some six or eight short, laconic poems, printed with plenty of white space around them, and a woodcut by my sister" (AE p. 234). The first *Prisma* issue contains an ultraist manifesto signed by Borges that criticizes traditional poets and labels long novels and poems as a waste of time; art should be freed by means of the metaphor. It also states that *Prisma*'s purpose is to make the new poetry available to a wide audience (RM p. 169). Guillermo de Torre describes the second issue as beginning with a "Proclama" that criticized the "tatuaje azul rubeniano," its "cachivaches ornamentales," and its "anecdotismo gárrulo." It stated that in contrast "nuestro arte quiere superar esas martingalas de siempre y descubrir facetas insospechadas al mundo." The purpose of ultraism was: "sintetizar la poesía en su elemento primordial: la metáfora. Cada verso de nuestros poemas posee su vida individual y representa una visión inédita."[3] Although this manifesto was signed by Borges, González Lanuza, Borges' cousin, and Guillermo de Torre, De Torre attributes it to Borges alone. The rest of this issue of *Prisma* contained Spanish ultraist poems (DT p. 116). In true vanguard style Borges and a group of his friends roamed the streets of Buenos Aires with pastepots and plastered the city's walls and buildings with their gift of culture. Luckily, Alfredo Bianchi, editor of the more prestigious magazine *Nosotros* saw a copy of *Prisma* and invited the young group of poets to submit an anthology of ultraist poetry for publication. This resulted in a December 1921 essay Borges wrote for *Nosotros* that defined the goals of ultraism for the benefit of Argentine and Spanish ultraist poets; the actual anthology of ultraist verse appeared in the September 1922 issue of *Nosotros* and included Borges' poem "Sábados" which was later published in *Fervor de Buenos Aires* (RM p. 170). Rodríguez Monegal gives prominence to the importance of Borges' belief in the non-existence of the individual ego as one of the principal motives for Borges' romance with ultraism whose goal—as Borges saw it—was the "transmutation of the world's concrete reality into an inner emotional reality" (RM p. 170). Soon after the demise of *Prisma*, Borges and his cohorts launched *Proa*; its first phase had three issues published between August 1922 and July 1923. The format was the same as that of the Madrid magazine *Ultra*—six pages that had the form of a three-paned mirror. Macedonio Fernández is hailed as one of the luminaries of the group of new poets. *Proa* also had a second phase with a different format, publishing fourteen-or-so issues beginning in August 1924 and ceasing publication in 1925 for lack of funds. Borges, Ricardo Güiraldes, Pablo Rojas Paz, and Brandán Caraffa launched this second phase of *Proa* (DT p. 116–117). Borges did most of the editing during *Proa*'s first phase; its first issue proclaimed a more eclectic view of ultraism: "Ultraism is not a sect designed as a prison." It can be seen as "an insatiable longing for faraway lands" or as an "exaltation of the metaphor" (RM p. 172). Also during this same time, Borges continued to write articles for *Nosotros* and *Inicial* (an avant-garde review) where he published an article on German expressionism and another criticizing the work of Leopoldo Lugones. Borges was now well launched into a career of editing and publishing (RM p. 172). Borges characterizes his feelings about these hectic years as follows:

> These years were quite happy ones because they stood for many friendships. There were those of Norah Lange, Macedonio Fernández, Piñero, and my father. Behind our work was a sincerity; we felt we were renewing both prose and poetry. (AE p. 235)

The friendship with Macedonio Fernández was especially important to Borges:

> We met on Saturday evenings at a café—the Perla, in the Plaza del Once. There we would talk till daybreak, Macedonio presiding. As in Madrid Cansinos had stood for all learning, Macedonio now stood for pure thinking. (AE p. 227)

Macedonio and Borges liked to discuss some of their mutual beliefs; key among them are the premises that we are all living in a dream world and that real truth is incommunicable. Borges' greatest debts to this new mentor include becoming a more skeptical reader and having a cultivated mind to use as a literary and intellectual sounding board.

Meanwhile, Borges' father's eyesight had taken a turn for the worse and he decided to return to Geneva to consult his doctor. All of this was bad timing from Jorge Luis' point of view since he was putting the finishing touches on *Fervor de Buenos Aires* and also had a crush on a young lady. This last circumstance inspired Borges to write several love-and-farewell poems to be included in *Fervor de Buenos Aires*; he had to accompany his father to Europe, due both to the closeness of the Borges' family circle and to the fact that Jorge Luis had never held a job in his life and had no means of supporting himself. Borges describes how *Fervor de Buenos Aires* was printed in a rush before his departure:

> I had bargained for sixty-four pages, but the manuscript ran too long and at the last minute five poems had to be left out—mercifully. I can't remember a single thing about them. The book was produced in a somewhat boyish spirit. No proofreading was done, no table of

contents was provided, and the pages were unnumbered. My sister made a woodcut for the cover, and three hundred copies were printed. (AE p. 224)

Borges' recently-developed friendship with Alfredo Bianchi, the publisher of *Nosotros*, resulted in a novel method of distribution for a good many of the copies of *Fervor de Buenos Aires*. Borges had his friend slip copies of the book into the pockets of the overcoats hanging in the cloakroom at the offices of *Nosotros*. The rest of the copies were just given away (AE p. 224–225). Borges characterizes the content of *Fervor de Buenos Aires* as follows:

> The book was essentially romantic, though it was written in a rather lean style and abounded in laconic metaphors. It celebrated sunsets, solitary places, and unfamiliar corners; it ventured into Berkeleyan metaphysics and family history; it recorded early loves. At the same time, I also mimicked the Spanish seventeenth century and cited Sir Thomas Browne's *Religio Medici* in my preface. I'm afraid the book was a plum pudding—there was just too much in it. (AE p. 225)

However, even at that time major critics saw *Fervor de Buenos Aires* in a more favorable light. Ramón Gómez de la Serna gave the book a very favorable review (April 24, 1924) in the prestigious *Revista de Occidente*, founded in the previous year by Ortega y Gasset. In addition, Enrique Díez-Canedo, a well-respected critic at that time, published a positive review of Borges' new book in the newspaper *España*; in it he states that Buenos Aires is more the "spiritual flame" of the poems rather than the actual theme of the book and that the poetry itself has a "classical" ring to it.[4]

During his stay in Spain, Borges published an article in two parts in the magazine *Alfar* (June-July 1924), and later republished it in *Inquisiciones* (1925), in which he still upholds the principal ultraist dogma: the key role of the metaphor in poetry. Borges postulates that metaphors are necessary to overcome the limitations inherent in ordinary language; he tries to classify metaphors and prove that they are less common in popular poetry (RM p. 181). Borges also published an article entitled "Quevedo's Grandeur and Defamation" (*Revista de Occidente*, Oct.-Dec. 1924) in which he admires Quevedo's metaphors, antitheses, adjectives, and the ability to go beyond physical reality and penetrate into a psychological reality; he identified with Quevedo as a man of intelligence and ideas. Borges sought to link Góngora with the symbolists, and Quevedo with the ultraists (RM p. 181–182). It is clear that Borges maintained a high level of interest in the intellectual, theoretical aspects of ultraism at least until his return to Buenos Aires in 1924. Nonetheless, the degree to which *Fervor de Buenos Aires* can be classified as ultraist is subject to debate; what the public man Borges was saying at that time in literary circles and writing in essays on literary theory stands in marked contrast to the actual contents of the poet Borges' first published poetic work. We find the paradox of Borges' poetic voice already negating ultraism and trying to liberate itself from its constraints, while simultaneously Borges the literary theorist is still churning out ultraist propaganda. Nowadays Borges agrees with his friend and translator from the French, Néstor Ibarra, who flatly stated that Borges stopped being an ultraist with the first ultraist poem he ever wrote. In his "Autobiographical Essay" Borges sums up his current feelings with regard to his involvement in the ultraist movement:

> I can only regret my early ultraist excesses. After nearly half a century,
> I find myself still striving to live down that awkward period of my life.
> (AE p. 227)

The mature Borges clearly wishes to disassociate himself as much as possible from his ultraist past; this desire resulted in direct and profound changes in the *Fervor de Buenos Aires* we read today. The original version containing forty-six poems is a collector's item that virtually no one ever sees or reads; Borges definitely prefers it to remain this way, and has done his best to surpress as much as possible the diffusion of this early material. The 1923 *Fervor de Buenos Aires* survives only in the hands of those fortunate enough to own one of the original three hundred copies; a few of the poems also live on in obscure out-of-print anthologies published in the 1920's and 1930's. The contents of *Fervor de Buenos Aires* next appears in print containing thirty-eight poems as part of *Poemas* (1922–1943) which Borges published in Buenos Aires in 1943. Eight poems were omitted from the 1923 version, two were retitled, four were lightly retouched, another dozen received moderate revisions, and twenty-two poems got a major overhaul. In *Poemas* (1923–1953), published in 1954, Borges again revised the contents of *Fervor de Buenos Aires*: one additional poem was omitted, eight received minor touch-ups, two got moderate revisions, two were changed extensively, and twenty-five were republished verbatim from the previous edition (1943). In 1958 *Poemas* (1923–1958) saw more changes in the contents of *Fervor de Buenos Aires*: one more poem was omitted, ten received minor changes, two received moderate revisions, and the remaining twenty-four poems were reprinted unscathed from the 1954 edition. *Obra poética 1923–1964* published in Buenos Aires in 1964 is the chronological terminus of this study and is the edition cited in all references to specific poems. In it Borges rejected one more poem leaving *Fervor de Buenos Aires* with a total of thirty-five poems; in addition, eleven poems received minor revisions, ten received moderate revisions, and somehow fourteen poems ran the gantlet untouched from the 1958 reprinting. However, this is not the end of this textual odyssey; *Obra poética 1923–1966* (Buenos Aires, 1966) pruned one more poem from *Fervor de Buenos Aires*, and gave minor touch-ups to seven and moderate revisions to two others. In the 1967 *Obra poética 1923–1967*, the 1966 version of *Fervor de Buenos Aires* is reprinted word for word except for printing errors. Despite his claims to the contrary in the preface, Borges gutted his 1964, 1966, and 1967 versions of *Fervor de Buenos Aires* with a republication of the work as a single, independent volume in 1969; he might have done well to give this work a new title to distinguish it from his previous work. Although Borges flatly states in the preface that he has not rewritten the book—"No he reescrito el libro. He mitigado sus excesos barrocos, he limado asperezas, he tachado sensiblerías y vaguedades . . ."[5]—the fact that he feels such an explanatory note is even necessary demonstrates his awareness that readers who are familiar with the previous texts contained in *Fervor de Buenos Aires* will notice substantial differences. It can also be seen as a ploy to discourage new readers from bothering to seek out the previous editions of the work.

Therefore, those wishing to savor the original spirit of *Fervor de Buenos Aires* are advised to use the revised, updated but not "mutilated" versions of 1964, 1966, or 1967. The 1969 "revision" suppressed three more poems and replaced them with two newly composed poems and one poem "plagiarized" from *El otro, el mismo*. In short, to say that the 1969 edition is a revised version of the 1964, 1966, and 1967 editions is an understatement bordering on dishonesty for it contains only *one* unchanged poem from those editions, four poems with minor changes, eight poems with moderate revisions, eleven poems with extensive revisions, and finally seven poems that were totally rewritten. At this point an exasperated reader may well ask which is the "real" or "definitive" text. Obviously, the question has no "correct" answer; it is left to each reader and critic to choose the edition that is most "suitable" or "appropriate" for a given purpose. Norman Thomas di Giovanni carefully documents all of these mutations through the year 1969 and quotes Borges as exclaiming upon the completion of those revisions that this was "just the way I want the poems to read," and then adding, "For a while, at least."[6]

Di Giovanni summarizes as follows some of the reasons for Borges' incessant penchant for revising his poetry:

> As a poet, Borges has striven over the years to write more and more clearly, plainly, and straightforwardly. A study of the revisions of his early work from edition to edition of the poems shows a stripping away of baroque ornament and a greater concern for natural word order and for the use of common language. Even his ideas about metaphor have moved in this direction. (SP p. xviii)

In this last sentence Di Giovanni should have said that it is *especially* Borges' ideas about metaphors that have changed; the desire to substitute simpler, less surprising metaphors for the more daring ultraist type was one of the principal drives behind Borges' desire to revise his previous work. Borges also sought to eliminate certain references to his personal life—especially his early love life—motivated by the desire both to preserve a greater degree of privacy and to increase the universal appeal of the poems. Carlos Meneses contends that with the 1923 publication of *Fervor de Buenos Aires*, Borges' desire to be associated with literary schools such as ultraism, his search for novelty, and his attempts to conform to national or international literary trends are already greatly diluted.[7] The process in which Borges will develop a highly original and independent poetic voice is already clearly in motion in the 1923 edition and accelerates with each subsequent one. In summary, the debate as to whether or not *Fervor de Buenos Aires* is ultraist poetry can be resolved in this manner: the original 1923 edition carries the strongest ultraist imprint; each subsequent revision increasingly divorces itself from its more ultraist ancestor to the point that by 1969 the tenor of the work cannot truly be called ultraist.

As a prelude to studying the poems, a careful reading of Borges' prefaces is very useful. In his original 1923 preface to *Fervor de Buenos Aires*, he defines the purpose of the book:

> I shall start out by observing that my poems, in spite of the misleading suggestion of their title, are not—nor did they for a single moment ever attempt to be—a compendium of the many aspects and places of my city. In this volume, Buenos Aires does not stand for the topographical convention implied by its name; it is my home, its familiar neighborhoods, and, along with them, what I experienced of love, of suffering, and misgivings. (SP p. 268)

Borges goes on to state that he deliberately left out elements that Buenos Aires shared with other port cities; instead he wanted to express "the amazement and the wonder of the places my long rambles lead me" and "the wonder of the streets deified by hope or by memory" (SP p. 268). Much of the rest of the preface represents a clear break with orthodox ultraist dogma. One of the techniques that Borges says he used in "several" pieces is the stringing out of metaphors which he sees as just one technique among many others. Although he confesses to enjoying "coining metaphors," Borges tells us that "I always put effectiveness before mere novelty," he also criticizes poets whose works consist of a piling of words on words and thus are reduced to little more than "showy trifles" (SP p. 269). In short, what Borges is saying in this 1923 preface is that the ultraist cult of the metaphor may produce pleasing esthetical games but is not the road to writing good poetry. The preface reveals that at this early stage Borges is well aware of the pitfalls inherent in blindly following the dogmas of literary schools and is determined to avoid them by blazing his own independent path. Perhaps Borges comes closest to summing up the contents of *Fervor de Buenos Aires* when he speaks of the poems as "intellectual adventures" that seek the magical links between today's man and his remotest origins.

In a final aside directed to the reader, entitled "A quien leyere" (included in some form in all subsequent editions of *Obra poética*), Borges alerts the reader to some of his basic philosophical premises:

> If the pages of this book offer some felicitous line or other, may the reader pardon me the discourtesy of having claimed it first. Our inconsequential selves differ but little; the circumstance that you are the reader and I the writer of these exercises is accidental and irrelevant. (SP p. 270)

Borges denies the existence and importance of the individual personality by telling us that one man is in some way all men, and that by extension the smallest part of anything necessarily implies the whole. This concept of the poet's work as an expression of the universal consciousness is the root of Borges' humility—he calls his poems mere "exercises." In truth many of Borges' poems are "exercises"; their clear purpose is to toy with one of the metaphysical problems or esthetic concepts that most preoccupy him. Through this process, the poet becomes the mirror of the universal truths in which the reader sees himself reflected. Also expressed here is Borges' view that there can truly be nothing new under the sun—all men repeat the rituals and acts of previous or future men. The poet's work is impoverished by the fact that he can only write down ideas and intentions that already have been expressed by others; nonetheless, much like Sisyphus, the poet is condemned to this fate and is resigned to it. "A quien leyere" also plays with the analogous idea that all literature is really one long book; this repeats the theme that writers only plagiarize from what has already been written or write something that someone else would have written anyway at some future date. Borges apologizes in advance to the reader for all such acts of "plagiarism."

In his preface to the 1964, 1966, and 1967 editions of *Obra poética*, Borges expands in more detail on some of these esthetic theories that try to define the role of the poet: "But all poetry is mysterious; nobody knows for sure what it has been given him to write" (SP p. 272). Borges clearly believes in the "muse" or some external force that compels him to write as he does. Borges' "poetic voice" takes on a certain degree of independence from the historical figure called Borges; the poet cannot claim total credit or responsibility for his own work. Borges then goes on to use some of his interpretation of Berkeley's metaphysics, using the apple-and-palate metaphor to describe the relationship between the poet and the reader:

> . . . poetry lies in the meeting of poem and reader, not in the lines of symbols printed on the page of a book. What is essential is the aesthetic act, the thrill, the almost physical emotion that comes with each reading. Maybe there is nothing new in this, but at my age novelties matter far less than truth. (SP p. 272)

Besides the obvious refutation of ultraism contained in the reference to "novelties," Borges tells us that poetry contained in books sitting on shelves for all practical purposes does not even exist. It is the reader who rediscovers the poem and gives it new life. To avoid oblivion, Borges constantly works to revise and improve his work in the hope that at least a few of his poems will surive in anthologies:

> One of three fates awaits a book of poetry: it may be relegated to oblivion, it may not leave behind a single line and yet give a sufficient picture of the man who wrote it, or it may bequeath a few poems to the anthologist. (SP p. 272)

Borges clearly wishes to avoid the fate of utter oblivion, and is not interested in having his poetry serve as some sort of dull documentation of the historical realities of the man called Borges. Instead, he modestly aspires to live on in a few of his finest works preserved in anthologies; in Borges' mind anthologies are akin to the encyclopedias which always fascinated him as depositories of the distilled essence of human achievements. In this manner, without directly stating it, Borges confesses to the reader that one of the forces that drives him to write poetry is this striving to attain a small measure of immortality through the atemporal life of his poetic persona, which can live on after the physical man Borges is gone forever.

The poetic persona or voice that manifests itself in *Fervor de Buenos Aires* appears to be radically different from the historical Borges who came back from Spain supposedly believing in the advent of a universal brotherhood among men (which implies a view of history as a linear progression), in ultraism and vanguard esthetic schools, and in novelty and modernity. It was a Borges who was interested in political systems, in participating in the somewhat superficial literary café life style, and in making propaganda to spread his esthetic credo. The poetic voice that speaks in Borges' first book either rejects or ignores all of this; the poetic persona in *Fervor de Buenos Aires* is introverted and insecure, seeking refuge in sheltered places, almost a desire to return to the safety of the womb. Furthermore this poetic voice has a circular view of history in which all ideas of human "progress"—political or social—become meaningless. Instead of praising revolutions in politics and literature and singing the praises of the universal brotherhood, the poetic voice dedicates itself to the study of basic metaphysical problems; it wonders about the ultimate meaning of human existence, seeks to discover the secret or lost links between man and the universe, and probes the mysteries of time's ebb.

Roland Barthes, while speaking of language and style, expresses the following ideas, which can shed light on the origins of Borges' poetic voice:

> . . . imagery, delivery, vocabulary spring from the body and the past of the writer and gradually become the very reflexes of his art. Thus under the name of style a self-sufficient language is evolved which has its roots only in the depths of the author's personal and secret mythology, that subnature of expression where the first coition of words and things takes place, where once and for all the great verbal themes of his existence come to be installed. Whatever its sophistication, style has always something crude about it: it is a form with no clear destination, the product of a thrust, not an intention, and, if it were, a vertical and lonely dimension of thought. Its frame of reference is biological or biographical, not historical: it is the writer's "thing" his glory and his prison, it is his solitude.[8]

In *Fervor de Buenos Aires* Borges' poetic voice can be seen as "thrusting" outward to assert itself along with all the themes that will consistently repeat themselves throughout Borges' literary career. Using Barthes' terminology, Borges' poetic voice is "a closed personal process," "indifferent to society," and not "the product of a choice or a reflection on literature"; "it rises up from the writer's myth laden depths and unfolds beyond his area of control" (RB p. 11). The author's poetic voice gradually develops a distinct life of its own, independent to some extent from the total control of the writer. Borges clearly believes in the concept of a literary persona that is separate from the writer; his piece entitled "Borges y yo" published in *El hacedor* devotes itself exclusively to this theme.

Also useful in this context is Barthes' view of literature as an onion rather than a piece of fruit with a central core. Following this line of thought, the literary work is not composed of a superficial outer skin and a fleshy inner portion that hides the secrets of the core, but rather the work should be seen as an onion with many successive layers or systems that are mutually dependent upon one another to form the whole, but do not lead up to or conceal any center point. From this vantage point, *Fervor de Buenos Aires* is composed of many layers of "onion skin." The book can be read literally as the contact of the man Borges with his native city after a long absence, it can be interpreted as the expression of a young man's first loves and frustrations, it can be read as a metaphysical tract that speculates on the problems associated with man's existence, and it can be read as an escapist work in which the author flees from the unpleasant realities of the industrialized modern world into a world of protective fantasies. All of these interpretations possess a certain validity, and none of them alone expresses the totality of the work; instead the layers of interrelated systems weave the fabric that represents the whole. The principal protagonist (or unifying thread) in *Fervor de Buenos Aires* that binds together the system-layers within the book is clearly time. The poetic voice tells us that the flow of time is the essence of man's being: it defines man and destroys him. Therefore, time and its relation to man is the key connection between the levels of interpretation of the poetry.

This study divides the poems of *Fervor de Buenos Aires* into thematic groups to facilitate a more careful examination of the content of the texts. These categories are neither rigid nor exclusive—many poems can be placed in several of the categories.

The largest category of poems can be called the "street" poems in have become the marrow of his being, the poet informs the reader that he has chosen the quiet outskirts of town as opposed to the busy downtown area as his principal setting:

> No las calles enérgicas
> molestadas de prisas y ajetreos,
> sino la dulce calle de arrabal
> enternecida de penumbra y ocaso[9]

In effect, quiet streets, shadows, and sunsets are the backdrop in the development of the entire work. Also hinted at in this poem is a fascination with the vast emptiness of the pampa that begins beyond the city's suburbs—a theme more thoroughly developed in the poem "La guitarra." The poet also states that the streets (positive symbols of protection) are the depositories of the hopes and illusions of the inhabitants whose interior lives are masked from casual view by the sheltering streets. The last lines both eulogize the streets and serve to give them a mythical, infinite quality:

> Hacia los cuatro puntos cardinales
> se han desplegado como banderas las calles;
> ojalá en mis versos enhiestos
> vuelen esas banderas. (OP p. 18)

The last two lines invoke the help of the muse in a manner similar to the medieval bard's custom of invoking divine inspiration. The poet also expresses his humility in these lines, fearing that the quality of the poetry might be insufficient for him to express himself adequately. The metaphor comparing the streets to unfurling flags is a holdover from his ultraist days in Spain; its function is to elevate to the level of an epic or a crusade what is to follow. The rest of the poems clearly lack this exhortative tone; however, "Las calles" is an appropriate piece in its context. It can be seen as the "hello" poem that greets the reader to the poetic experience that is to follow, just as the last or "good-bye" poem "Despedida" serves as the completion of the borgesian circle.

"La Plaza San Martín" is a good next stop in this street odyssey through Buenos Aires. The plaza's function is to serve as a dam where time's flow can be stopped, or at least temporarily checked: "la tarde toda se había remansado en la plaza" (OP p. 25). The late afternoon is the time chosen for the visit because it is when evening's shadows begin to blur reality's sharp edges. Then, all feeling recedes as the trees grant absolution from worldly cares: "Todo sentir se aquieta / bajo la absolución de sus árboles." The plaza's statue connects the heavenly and earthly planes, and all is peace and harmony:

> ¡Qué bien se ve la tarde
> desde el fácil sosiego de los bancos! (OP p. 26)

Then the poet introduces a note of consciousness of an external reality in a reference to the port as a lure to distant places, but the dominant theme is that of the square as a quiet oasis where timeless illusion flourishes.

"El jardín botánico" is the setting (or pretext) chosen for a poem on man's alienation from his fellow men. After a somewhat rhetorical beginning in which the tree's branches are seen reaching into the heavens in search of links with the divine, the poet compares the isolation of each tree in a forest with man's isolation from his fellow beings: one is surrounded by them, yet totally alone. This fundamental aloneless produces anguish in each human being, and in turn is but a faint reflection of the original anguish felt by God, an anguish that has not been quenched by "la infinita profusión de estrellas, almas, voces / y ocasos" (OP p. 24); all of these items may populate and crowd the universe but provide little solace to gods and men. Time appears as "garrulous" by providing an infinite procession of fleeting stars, souls, and sunsets. As the poet steps out of the botanical garden, he is taken aback by a group of little girls; in one of them he already sees the young woman that time's flow would transform her into. Both the botanical garden and the street incident serve as backgrounds to the interior emotional-metaphysical world that the poetic persona is trying to create. Here, Borges is following a little fragment of his own ultraist theory in the poem by taking the elements of the outside world of reality and forging them into his own inner emotional reality.

One of the finest "street poems" is entitled "Carnicería" in which the poet transforms in ultraist style the ordinary into the fantastic, giving the reader a new perspective on a commonplace but seldom-thought-about reality. The butcher shop, more vile than a whorehouse, is an affront to the dignity of the street; the cow's-head image decorating the doorway presides like an idol over the pagan rites of a strange witches' sabbath in which chunks of meat are displayed on marble (tomb-like) slabs.

"Barrio reconquistado" is another attempt to see the commonplace in a novel fashion. The habitual beauty of the streets is not appreciated until people are denied use of them by a fierce storm that "humiliates the houses" (the poet uses violent Christian imagery to depict the storm: "dolorido en contorsión de mártir" [OP p. 31]). When the storm abates, the people "reconquer" the streets attracted by the rainbow and sensual smell of the wet ground:

> y en las hojas lucientes que ilustran la arboleda
> dijo su trémula inmortalidad el estío. (OP p. 31)

Summer's false immortality is as fragile as the trembling water droplets left on the tips of the leaves. Again the reader is reminded of time's flow, for even the seasons must die to be later reborn.

One of the poet's favorite areas of the city are the last streets of the town—the transition from city to country which can also symbolize a cornucopia of dualities such as heaven/earth, reality/fantasy, and limited space/infinity. In "Arrabal" the poet's feet, like the last houses at the city's edge, refuse to go beyond the border that separates them from the infinite empty space beyond. In this transition zone grass grows between the stones in the street: man is seen in conflict with the infinite which he battles by creating his sheltered world of boundaries and limits. The poet realizes the vanity of this by calling the setting of the sun a daily failure—as the sun fails to stop the flow of time and must also follow a cycle of death and rebirth, man is also a failure in his attempt to control the infinite universe with his finite tools. Nonetheless, the poet feels that his fate and literary voice are intricately related—past, present and future—with this one set of limits called Buenos Aires. This sunset revelation on the edge of the city has a definite mystical quality.

The most graphic "outskirts poem" is "Sur" (most likely

referring to the Santelmo and Montserrat neighborhoods found to the south of downtown Buenos Aires). The scene is set, of course, at sunset when both people and light abandon the streets leaving the poet alone with the passing trains to form his personal vision. Through the poet's eyes the reader sees these tumbled-down, poor Buenos Aires suburbs pierced and dominated by railyards. The imagery is military; through the ennumeration of stark images the poet creates his battlefield-like vision of the scarred neighborhood—all of which leaves a bitter taste in his soul. In poems such as this one, Borges approaches what could be called "social" poetry—an insinuated commentary on poor living conditions and the desecration of the environment by technological advances.

In "La guitarra," the Pampa—mysterious and awe-inspiring—is seen to spring to life from the back of a house's patio at the edge of Buenos Aires. Borges clearly prefers to view this grandeur from the protected vantage point offered by the patio; it is a sheltered place from which to contemplate the timeless world of the infinite. The guitar music is the catalyst that reveals a multi-level vision of the pampa contained in the mythical space briefly created by the music. On one level the poet sees the immense space of the pampa, once the scene of violent Indian raids, now quiet and "tired" where cattle peacefully graze. On another plane, the pampa is seen as representing the infinite void of the universe—a place where God can walk unrestrained by physical limits and where the smallness of man and his creations is evident. Finally, another personal vision surges forth in which the guitar's notes conjure up visions of a current love affair. Brusquely, in cataclysmic fashion, the music ends, the vision ceases, mythical time and space is banished, and life's routine resumes its usual monotony; however, for at least a few moments, the poet and reader escape from reality's iron grasp. The conciseness of the language makes the poem effective: the guitar player is never mentioned—he is reduced to a right hand plucking strings. This is an example of the "essential poetry" the poet strives to write.

Although a great many of the poems contained in *Fervor de Buenos Aires* have a "crepuscular quality," four poems in particular can be called "sunset" poems. The first of them, "Calle desconocida" has a "soft" sunset theme; the poem begins with incorrect information which Borges later noticed but chose not to correct in subsequent editions:

> Penumbra de la paloma
> llamaron los hebreos a la iniciación de la tarde (OP p. 21)

The Hebrews actually associated the dove with the dawn and the crow with sunset; the crow—often used as a symbol of evil or doom—was inappropriate in this context. Therefore, Borges decided to leave the reference to the dove intact—it clearly symbolizes peace and harmony in this poem. Here the sunset is seen not as a symbol of man's essential nothingness, but rather as "una música esperada"—a peaceful repetition of established harmonies. Enjoying this moment, the poet discovers a new, wide street that blends with its soft colors into the frame of the sunset. The scene struck the poet as unusual at that instant when the sun's dying rays gave this street a particular appeal that it would have lacked under ordinary circumstances; "haciéndola real como una leyenda o un verso" (OP p. 22). The sunset's glow makes the street "real" like a legend or a line of poetry. Thus, in a matter-of-fact conversational tone, the poet states a radical idea: the world of poetry and myth—both out of time's flow—are more real than objective reality. The poet uses the word "milagro"—miracle—to describe the surging forth of this poetic intuition of a profound truth whose catalyst was an ordinary sunset on a seemingly ordinary street. After this incident, the poet is able to decipher more of the mystery behind that sunset; using the Cansinos-Asséns image of the candelabra, the poet sees the life of each individual as an isolated flame. Man's inability to communicate effectively with his fellow men and to bring to consciousness the content of his subliminal memory blinds him to another profound truth: each man is all men. Using Christian imagery as a tool, the poet reminds us that man blindly treads on his fellows' "Gologothas" or *via crucis*, unmindful that as he walks over the sacred ground of others he is merely repeating their steps in an endless cycle of ritual.

In "Ultimo resplandor," the poet again tells us that the brief sunset moments are the best time to capture poetic, atemporal intuitions. The dream-like quality of the setting sun creates a magical world of illusion which darkness finally snuffs out like a dream destroyed by the sleeper's awakening. The darkness has a violent quality here—it imposes its fears upon man, who struggles to maintain his illusions. The poem "Atardeceres" also brings in the violent, destructive aspect of the darkness; darkness defeats the "mutilated" afternoon's vain colors and becomes the blood of wounded things:

> La oscuridá es la sangre
> de las cosas heridas. (OP p. 66)

The content of the poem itself is a collection of disconnected incidents. First the mood is established by the sunset whose glow makes the street go beserk and open itself up to random dreams. Meanwhile, the poets' wanderings are softened and blessed by a grove of trees until the birds become silent and the last ray of sunshine is banished by the night. The guitar represents an absence of love; the poet now hears a tale of love's disillusion and pain. It is then that the silent darkness becomes blood—that of the afternoon and that of the poet's own tortured soul.

In "Campos atardecidos" the sunset is seen as a painful wound not yet having formed a scab on the body of the afternoon. It is technically the weakest poem in the "sunset series," for it is composed of a string of ultraist metaphors and lacks a clear focus. Three of the ultraist metaphors ("El poniente de pie como un Arcángel / tiranizó el camino," "Las esquilas recogen la tristeza / dispersa de la tarde," and "La luna nueva / es una vocecita desde el cielo") are reworked material taken from poems previously published in Spanish literary magazines and juxtaposed here with dubious success. In the poem, the countryside again invades the town at dusk, and we are reminded that time gives the appearance of being slowed and "fatigued" during this transition period between the cycles of day and night. Finally night's darkness will "shut down" the mirrors—a clear reference to the end of this brief period of illusion. Although this poem lacks technical finesse by showing us a stream of metaphors much like a proud child would show off his new toys, it is redeemed by the esthetic thrill Borges speaks of in his preface to the work. Indeed, these intellectual "toys" are pleasing, especially ones such as his description of how night banishes the colors of the objects around us:

> Los colores temblando se acurrucan
> en las entrañas de las cosas. (OP p. 67)

"Caminata," although not directly related to the sunset poems, can be mentioned here as the finest night poem in *Fervor de Buenos Aires*; the sun has long since set and the poet wanders alone through the deserted streets over which he now exercises more "jurisdiction." In a tone of utter calm, his own solitude and that of the night—composed of shadow, simple geometric forms, and the people's instinctive fear of the dark—share the view of this urban landscape. The light breeze brings in hints of pleasant country plant aromas that make the live earth stir with longing beneath its asphalt prison. The clocks break the silence at midnight, spilling forth a wonderfully generous swath of slow-moving time in which all dreams become possible, (in stark contrast to time's hectic, demeaning pace during the daylight hours). "Caminata" is clearly an escape poem in which the poet finds peaceful solace from the day's tensions and cares in the night's comforting, silent shadows. The night is useful because it masks reality; time's flow is arrested somewhat, the poet can fantasize among the pleasant geometric shapes formed by the shadows, gaze at the twinkling street lights and the stars, and play intellectual games. The poet brings in a bit of Berkeley with the idea that the deserted street would cease to exist if he were not there to conjure it up mentally. The last seven lines of the poem have a different tone and can be interpreted as a eulogy of the grandeur of the night seen as an angel whose wings obscure the daylight; thus, this violent Christian imagery resurfaces, used for esthetic, not religious purposes. Finally, the night loses the ordinary city streets in a backwash of time, in a corner of nothingness; the city is covered by immense, sterile, infinite space.

The cemeteries are the next stop in the poet's wanderings through his city. There are four of these "cemetery" or death-theme poems in *Fervor de Buenos Aires*. The best one is "*La recoleta*"; the poem's title refers to the Buenos Aires cemetery in which the poet himself expects to be buried someday. The poet asks what meaning can life possibly have if all men and their works must die:

> Convencidos de caducidad,
> irrealizados por tanta certidumbre de anulación, . . . (OP p. 19)

The park-like, peaceful cemetery prefigures man's eventual fate. The substance of the tomb monuments is vanity; "hecha de mármol, de rectitud, y sombra interior" (OP p. 19); this description of the tombs mirrors the state of the corpses within: cold as marble, stiff and straight, and dwelling in eternal darkness. The poet tells us that man needs dreams, illusions, and indifference to cope with the imposing reality of his own death. Only life truly exists because death, time, and space are all creations of man's imagination:

> son instrumentos mágicos del alma,
> y cuando ésta se apaga,
> juntamente se apagan el espacio, el tiempo, la muerte, (OP p. 20)

When the soul dies, so do time, space, and death; they are nothing but man-invented concepts, which are illusions that disappear like the images reflected in a mirror when light ceases. The poet ponders the mystery of human existence, and then abruptly changes the tone of quiet meditation. The last three lines read like a tombstone epitaph and have a choppy rhythm that separates them from the rest of the poem and serves to hammer home to the reader once again the basic theme: all men die. "Remordimiento por cualquier defunción" sees in the death of one man the death of all men. In this vision death for the deceased person is seen as the loss and absence of the world; his abandoned booty of streets, patios, and thoughts is quickly snapped up by the living who thus become "thieves":

> nos hemos repartido como ladrones
> el asombroso caudal de noches y días. (OP p. 40)

There are two tombstone-epitaph poems in this "cemetery series"; "Inscripción sepulcral" uses autobiographical data to make a statement about death and heroes. On the most basic level this poem can be read as a hymn of praise to Borges' mother's grandfather, and as an example of Borges' fascination with "men of action." On another level the poem can be interpreted as merely using the autobiographical data as a framework to make a philosophical statement: heroes die like all other men and time reduces their bodies and their deeds to dust. The poem begins in a flowery, declamatory style; short sentences ending with periods at the end of several of the lines give the poem a choppy rhythm that rises in a crescendo ending with the next-to-last line, which serves as a bridge between the towering heights of the beginning of the poem and the nothingness in which it ends. In this masterfully constructed poem, the hero receives lavish praise in the first seven lines, dies "beseiged" by exile in the eighth line, and is reduced to ashes in the ninth and final line.

"Inscripción en cualquier sepulcro" closes the "cemetery cycle" of poems; it succinctly summarizes Borges' view of death. Men should not waste their effort trying to eternalize names, opinions, events, and patriotic verbiage by etching them into marble inscriptions: "Tanto abalorio bien adjudicado está a la tiniebla" (OP p. 42). Borges denies the validity of any cult to the hero by maintaining that the external facts of one's life are best forgotten. The essentials of a man's life—hope, pain, pleasure—are immortal and do not require any effort to preserve:

> Lo esencial de la vida fenecida
> —la trémula esperanza,
> el milagro implacable del dolor y el asombro del goce—
> siempre perdurará (OP p. 42)

The poet concludes that it is foolish to seek the immortality of the soul when we ourselves are already the immortality of the men who lived before us and future men will provide our own immortality. In short, one man is all men.

Another group of poems can be called the "protected space" poems; "Un patio" is representative of their tone. In it the poet shows his preference for sheltered places; places like the patio become womb-like havens to which the poet can retreat and escape from objective reality. On another plane, the patio represents controlled space as opposed to infinite space which the poet often finds frightening. In addition, the poet sees the patio as a zone of transition between the highly protected limited space of the home and the infinite universe that surrounds it. In the patio the poet sees the universe in microcosm, with all of its elements in manageable harmony:

> Lindo es vivir en la amistad oscura
> de un zaguán, de una parra y de un aljibe. (OP p. 30)

Confined man-made space (zaguán), cultivated plants (parra) and a flowing of water tamed by man (aljibe) compose this artificial mini-universe; the adjective "oscura" might best be translated as "sheltered and mysterious" which are words that sum up the patio's overall effect.

The poem "Jardín" contrasts a barren scarred landscape with the tranquil harmony of the garden; here the protected space of the garden represents an oasis of peace, order, and spiritual hope within the chaos of the infinite universe symbolized by the "sterile hills" and "sad," "uselessly green" sea. The garden is described as "una luz apacible / que ilumina la tarde"; its impact is summed up by the last two lines:

> El jardincito es un día de fiesta
> en la eternidad de la tierra. (OP p. 41)

Again we see controlled space, tamed by man, contrasted with and surrounded by the harsh, uncontrollable forces of an infinite universe.

The "protected space" is also evident in "Cercanías" in which the patio is seen as the transitional point between the heavens and earth and also the point of contact between the center of family tradition—represented by the home—and the world of other men beyond, which is represented by the city streets. The balance of the poem is an ennumeration of other such favorite sheltered vantage points upon which the poet showers heart-felt tenderness; they include windows with grill work from which the same segment of the street can be repeatedly and safely contemplated, dark bedrooms with shiny mahogany furniture (a womb-like retreat), and certain street intersections of surburban city neighborhoods from which the infinite emptiness beyond can be safely viewed. Finally, the comparision of the mirror with a dammed up pool in the shadows alerts the reader to another function of these protected places: they all slow the passage of time—their stability or repetitive sameness deny the flow of time.

The poem "Sala vacía" expands upon this theme of stopping time's flow with controlled spaces, but comes to the conclusion that the attempt is basically a failure. The heavy mahogany furniture, fading upholstry, and daguerreotypes of long-dead ancestors that decorate the walls of the living room fight a losing battle with time. Although they try to maintain the illusion of a perpetual present in the enclosed space of the living room, the noise from the street seeps in along with the sun's penetrating rays that "humiliate" the old armchairs and corner and choke to death the ancestor's ghostly remnants. Bright light and noise dispel the illusion of timeless, protected space which can only exist in quiet, dark places such as shuttered rooms of the home, the patio, and the garden.

"La vuelta" is yet another poem in which the poet longs for the protectiveness of familiar surroundings. He has returned to a once-familiar residence after a long absence and finds that the house and its garden no longer "recognize" him. The anguished poet speculates as to how long it will take to "retame" this once-familiar spot with daily routine. The poem is perhaps the most poignant example of the poet's urgent need for a protected vantage point from which to contemplate a disturbingly disorderly universe; the constant use of the first person accentuates the immediate, personal, confessional quality of the work.

Five of the poems in *Fervor de Buenos Aires* deal directly with the book's principal protagonist—time. "El truco"—the name of an Argentine card game—shows how ritualistic behavior can displace the ordinary flow of time with the atemporal world of myth. The first line sums up the basic premise: "Cuarenta naipes han desplazado la vida." In the middle of the poem this theme is restated: "En los lindes de la mesa / el vivir común se detiene" (OP p. 27). The words "amuletos" and "exorcismo" conjure up thoughts of ancient and primitive religious rites; the card players recapture past times and become one with all men who have repeated this same ceremony ("los jugadores en fervor presente / copian remotas bazas" [OP p. 28]). The poet repeats his idea that one man is all men and that the lives of those living in present time immortalizes at least in some small way those who have already died. The theme of the universe being governed by a series of constantly repeating cycles (el eterno retorno) is also clearly present in the poem. Closed systems—such as the strict rules that govern the card game—create their own small cosmos in which men can happily forget time's inexorable flow. However, the poet knows that all such attempts are "brillantes embelecos" doomed to failure. "El truco" has some fine imagery; the reader can clearly see and hear "el siete de oros tintineando esperanza" (OP p. 27). In short, this is one of the finest pieces in *Fervor de Buenos Aires* because of its unusually well-realized interrelation of structure and content.

The poem "Vanilocuencia" picks up the theme of the futility of the effort to halt time's flow: "Siempre hay otros ocasos, otra gloria" (OP p. 32). Here the weapon used to fight time is poetry itself, because poetry—like the card game—represents a ritualistic activity; it is a closed system with its own internal structure, and therefore can be a refuge from the onward rush of time. The poet is revealing one of the purposes of his book: to slow time with literary creations—closed systems that are atemporal. The poet asks himself, rhetorically, why he persists in the effort to halt time with poetry when he knows that the very subject matter of his poems is constantly suffering time's permutations. His street and house cry out their newness each day and appear as yet unkissed lips: "Nuevas / como una boca no besada" (OP p. 32). Again, the poet recognizes that the battle against time is fruitless, but it is his fate and duty to continue the fight until he too must inevitably succumb to time's ravages. Borges provides some additional insight on his concept of time in his essay "Nueva refutación del tiempo":

> And yet, and yet . . . Negar la sucesión temporal, negar el yo, negar el universo astronómico, son desesperaciones aparentes y consuelos secretos. Nuestro destino (a diferencia del infierno de Swedenborg y del infierno de la mitología tibetana) no es espantoso por irreal; es espantoso porque es irreversible y de hierro. El tiempo es la substancia de que estoy hecho. El tiempo es un río que me arrebata, pero yo soy el río; es un tigre que me destroza, pero yo soy el tigre; es un fuego que me consume, pero yo soy el fuego. El mundo, desgraciadamente, es real; yo, desgraciadamente, soy Borges.[10]

It is an error to see the poem "Rosas" as only a political poem about a nineteenth-century dictator; here again, the principle theme is clearly time. The historical figure "Rosas" is used as mere historical raw material to weave the fabric of the poem; the reader should not confuse the spool of thread with the finished garment. The setting for reminiscence of times gone by is a quiet drawing room where the clock pours forth nonadventurous, unexciting, present time; even the "red passion" of the heavy mahogany furniture is dead. Then, someone mentions the name of the dictator which causes dark memories to stir in the minds of those present. The poet then sums up the Rosas' entire career in four magnificent lines that say more than a whole volume of biography:

> Famosamente infame
> su nombre fue desolación en las calles,
> idolátrico amor en el gauchaje
> y horror de puñaladas en la historia. (OP p. 36)

Nonetheless, Rosas' crimes against humanity are slowly being forgotten and are, indeed small when compared to those commited by the worst offender of all—time, which destroys all. The poet uses violent imagery—blood, wounds—to show that time is a far worse criminal than any murderous dictator such as Rosas. The poet reduces the gigantic figure of the anti-hero Rosas to the level of an ordinary person like himself or the reader—a mere fact sprinkled at random into the clogged annals of history:

> creo que fue como tú y yo
> un azar intercalado en los hechos
> que vivió en la cotidiana zozobra
> e inquietó para felicidades y penas
> la incertidumbre de otros. (OP p. 37)

In this perceptive view of the dictator in history, the poet refers to the "sea" that separates him from present time and contemporary men. This is both a reference to the fact that Rosas was buried abroad and to the large expanse of time that separates Rosas' reality from us. Indeed, this "sea" is so wide that even God has probably forgotten the dictator and the poorest and least of men now trample over his grave and his memory. In the last three masterfully written lines the poet tells us that those who now hate the dictator are really offering alms to his "impoverished" memory and are thus helping to delay his utter oblivion:

> y es menos una injuria que una piedad
> demorar su infinita disolución
> con limosnas de odio. (OP p. 37)

Holidays as ritualistic behavior designed to deal with the problem of time are the theme of two poems: "Final de año" and "La noche de San Juan." In "Final de año" we learn that man does not celebrate the New Year's coming because of the calendar or the "sterile" metaphor of the cycle of death and rebirth, or because of astronomical considerations; instead, the holiday is a commemoration of the enigma of passing time and how it effects our lives. It is a realization of the "miracle" or strange paradox that because of its constant and dependable flow, time is the only stable factor in man's existence: it is simultaneously immobile (constant) and flowing. The purpose of "La noche de San Juan" is to give a fresh perspective to this now Christian holiday with clear pagan roots that celebrates the longest day of the year and the beginning of summer. The quiet soft twilight is broken by the crackling rhythms (compared to guitar music) of the shooting red flames; there is violent pagan imagery that compares the wood being burned to the bodies of sacrificial victims which shed their blood to feed the flames. Christian imagery completes this vignette with the "holy" night praying on rosary beads composed of the stars scattered about the heavens.

Three poems in *Fervor de Buenos Aires* can be called "philosophical poems"; they include "Amanecer," "Benarés," and "Llaneza." "Llaneza" contains the most concise summary of Borges' personal philosophy of life to be found in *Fervor de Buenos Aires*. The poet leads the reader from the garden gate into the protected world represented by the home and surrounding yard. This hallowed place is refuge where the poet is accepted at once without question as one of the elements that make up a harmonious whole; nothing is demanded of him in this special space—his essence, including his defects and eccentricities, are known and accepted. The poet need not play any roles and does not have to be on guard to protect himself from the prying intrusions of outsiders. We are told that heaven should be a place such as this—a feeling of total peace. The poet reveals to the reader the way to achieve happiness and peace in life: one must identify and understand one's proper niche in the universe, accept it, be happy in that role, and co-exist in harmony with all else, realizing that each individual is but one tiny limited element of a greater whole. The reader is advised not to seek "victories" or the praise of his fellow men:

> sino sencillamente ser admitidos
> como parte de una Realidad innegable,
> como las piedras y los árboles. (OP p. 56)

In "Amanecer" the poet philosophizes while roaming the streets of Buenos Aires in the stillness of the night; here the night represents peace, rest, and the dream world created by the poet. The dawn with its glaring light will show harsh realities—the slums and the dreary existence that their inhabitants lead. The poet would prefer to think that the night's dream world is truly the real world and that the daylight world is nothing but an illusion. The poet uses the last moments of darkness before dawn to play with the philosophy of Schopenhauer and Berkeley; in this esthetic vision the poet sees Buenos Aires as a collective dream conjured up by its inhabitants. When most men are asleep, the city's delicate web of fantasy is maintained by a few night owls. Then, the poet mixes in some gnostic thought into this just-created esthetic toy: in these pre-dawn hours so few men are awake to create the world mentally that a mischievous god could easily destroy the universe. However, ugly reality imposes itself again with the arrival of dawn and the poet's esthetic toy is dispelled by the morning sun's bright rays. The poet regrets that he too is an accomplice in this new defeat of the world of illusion, for he too helps to recreate his share of the city by thinking of his house and returning to it at daybreak. Also repeated here is the theme of the use of mental activity to stop the flow of time and to replace objective reality with a more pleasant one; the poet knows these attempts must necessarily end in failure, but keeps trying nonetheless.

"Benarés" is the quintessence of the philosophical "esthetic toy" poem. Whereas in "Amanecer" the existence of the city of Buenos Aires was maintained by dreams, in "Benarés" the poet creates his own city in the fantasy world of the mind. The city is a dense illusion like that of a whole garden reflected in a mirror; the houses stretch out to infinity like a mouth that repeats ceaseless prayer litanies. Violent imagery predominates, highlighting the sharp contrasts between light and shadow; the sunlight is savage like a tiger's claws that rip into the shadows of interior spaces (temples, prisons, stables, patios). In addition, the sun squeezes drunken colors from the walls and produces shoulder-burdening heat. In the oppressive heat the city "pants" and spreads to the horizon like concentric waves caused by a stone thrown into a pond. The sounds of the surrounding animal-filled jungles and their heavy odors evoke exotic mystery. The vision of the jungle crashes into the dawn along with the mournful-sounding cries of the muezzin. However, the individual inhabitants of the city are seen only in their footsteps and dreams. After creating this masterful vision, the poet marvels aloud to the reader that the city he has evoked with his halting metaphors really exists in all of its putrid reality—symbolized by the corpses that lie in the streets. In this case the created world of illusion closely approximates a reality—a "proof" that man can reduce reality to his own representation of it. However, the poet could just as well have named the poem "Uqbar" or "Orbis Tertius" because its purpose is to be a pleasure-producing esthetic experience; it is an intellectual game or "toy" and not a poem about a real city in India.

For those critics who keep asking Borges in published interviews why he never writes any love poems, it should be noted here that there are five love poems in *Fervor de Buenos Aires*. The most direct of these is "Sábados" which Borges dedicated to his current love at that time—Concepción Guerrero. In later editions her identity shrinks to the initials "C.G.," due both to Borges' desire for personal privacy and to the fact that her actual identity is of little interest nowadays since Borges lost all romantic feelings for her shortly after writing the poem. The poem is divided into four parts that represent distinct poetic moments. The first part sets the romantic mood with the presence of the loved one compared to sweet incense whose rich fragrance can later be recalled. Christian imagery predominates: the sun "redeems" the humiliated streets, and desires nailed into the air by the piano are "uncrucified." Whereas the first section is filled with the beauty of the loved one, the second speaks of "desamor" and the suffering involved with loving someone. The poet negates himself; he is nothing in comparison with the beauty of the loved one despite the fact that his love sometimes is unrequited:

> Ya casi no soy nadie,
> Soy tan sólo un deseo
> que se pierde en la tarde.
> En ti está la delicia
> Como está la crueldad en las espadas. (OP p. 61)

The third moment of the poem is a drawing-room scene; night has enveloped the house and the lovers sit silently while her modesty, his desire, and anguish all speak their inner language. There are two especially erotic lines:

> Sobrevive a la tarde
> la blancura gloriosa de tu carne. (OP p. 61)

The fourth section is a one-sentence, somewhat trite love confession; nothing could be further away from ultraism.

In "Trofeo" the poet uses both sea and musical imagery to describe the profound effect that one privileged day of contemplating his love's beauty has had upon him. He bids her farewell at dusk and while walking home through familiar streets that still hold her image, he becomes sad upon thinking that only one or two impressions of this joyful day with his love can be saved like trophies, for the rest of this day's memories will soon be totally effaced by time.

The poem "Ausencia" is one Borges' most moving love poems. It speaks with unconsolable grief about the dissolution of a relationship. The poet's life is in shambles and now must be rebuilt stone by stone. However, memories of his former lover persist doggedly into the present and cannot be surpressed. He sees the absent person in the sunsets, in music, in certain words, and places that once brought to mind pleasant shared memories; they have lost their meaning and now produce pain. Even the heavens participate in his feeling of loss with their repeated "clamor." The absence is compared to a terrible sun that never sets and whose constant penetrating rays produce great pain:

> ¿En qué hondonada empozaré mi alma
> donde no pueda vigilar tu ausencia
> que como un sol terrible, sin ocaso,
> brilla, definitiva e inclemente? (OP p. 55)

In the last two desperate lines the poet feels strangled by the absence of his lover as if he had a tight noose around his neck. This poem, in the first person, with its openly confessional tone is a poignant catharsis of strong emotions.

"Forjadura" is another "pain-of-love" cartharsis poem. In fact, the poet tells us that one of the functions of writing poetry is to create an outlet for such emotion. Like a blind person he gropes for the proper words for his poetry: he wants his bonfire of words to burn brightly on the "flagellated" back of time. The fuel for this poetic fire is composed of the poet's deepest preoccupatons and anguish:

> He de encerrar el llanto de las tardes
> en el duro diamante del poema. (OP p. 64)

Upon sealing his exorcised pain and troubles in the "diamond of the poem," the poet aludes to the fact that omissions and what is not directly stated can often be more richly explanatory than detailed descriptions: "en lo callado se embravece un grito." In Borges' subsequent poetry collections, he is more faithful to this credo: as the years go by his personal life will surface in his poetry in the form of very hard "diamonds" into which only more perceptive readers will penetrate. The poet concludes the work with the belief that his having once loved redeems him in a large measure from his current desolate state, and that the "night" in which he finds himself is fertile ground for the sowing of verses. In "Forjadura" the poet tells us why he writes: to combat the flow of time, to purge himself of strong emotions, to push aside barriers, and to get a glimpse of other worlds that transcend everyday reality.

"Despedida," the last poem in *Fervor de Buenos Aires*, has a double function. First, it is the "good-bye" poem that bids the reader farewell just as the first poem—"Las calles"—serves to begin this cycle of poetry with its welcome greeting. The poem "Despedida" also has a second clear function: it was born out of a concrete biographical circumstance. Borges was forced to abandon a love affair due to his return to Europe with his family in 1923. The reference to three hundred nights represents the approximate length of his absence. The poem really serves as a triple farewell: to his lover, to his city, and to the reader. The poet sums up his feelings in these three lines:

>El tiempo arrancará con dura mano
>las calles enzarzadas en mi pecho.
>No habrá sino recuerdos. (OP p. 68)

The poem is neatly divided into three sections. The problem (forced absence) is briefly stated in the first three lines. The second section begins with the three-line summing-up noted above that describes how the poet will be affected; the rest of this development section is devoted to a declamatory segment in parentheses in a confessional tone. The third and final section of the poem is a two-line summary that expresses the irremediable sadness that the poet will feel during this period of absence. It is an appropriate ending to the work and to this tour of the poet's inner emotional reality.

In summary, it is evident that *Fervor de Buenos Aires* is not a book of poems about the city of Buenos Aires. Any city could have been chosen to provide the backdrop for the content of the book. However, by chosing Buenos Aires (rather than Madrid or Geneva, for example) the poet has come to terms with his destiny—he is a twentieth-century man, born and raised in Buenos Aires, Argentina, and will use the Spanish language as his principal vehicle for literary expression. The youth with illusions of unlimited horizons is gone; the poet with calm resignation accepts the external limitations imposed upon him by his personal circumstances and his place in history. Nonetheless, this recognition of his limits gives the poet a clear identity and sense of freedom and of purpose that the youth of the Madrid cafés lacked. The young man that returned from Spain touting avant-garde literary and political ideas is not the poetic voice heard in *Fervor de Buenos Aires*. Instead, what is revealed by the texts is a poetic persona who has rejected all literary and political dogma. The poet sees ultraist, expressionist, and other contemporary literary trends as tools that sometimes can be used effectively to pursue his own literary ends. When such techniques detract or are irrelevant to the task at hand, they are replaced by more effective tools. The poet is interested in using whatever technique will best express his inner reality. This further clarifies the reason why Buenos Aires is not the centerpiece of the work: *Fervor de Buenos Aires* deals with inner emotional and intellectual realities; it is a work concerned with inner, personal space rather than outer, collective space. Since poetry is the vehicle used to forge this inner world, the work might have been more accurately entitled *Fervor de la poesía*; through these poems the poet comes to terms with himself and finds his safe niche in a vast, disorderly universe.

The book has a definite escapist tone: the poet replaces a disagreeable external reality with more manageable and rewarding inner realitites. The poetic persona evidenced in *Fervor de Buenos Aires* has rejected all notions of man's technological and social "progress," hence, his lack of interest in political systems and applied science. The poet has adopted a circular view of history in which man merely repeats recurring patterns of behavior rather than constantly blazing new trails in linear fashion. In this cosmovision, true novelty is impossible; therefore the futility of the main thrust of the turn-of-the-century political, social, and literary movements is made manifest; their key premises were based on a firm belief in change, that "modern" men could "improve" themselves and transform the universe. Since the poetic persona in *Fervor de Buenos Aires* rejects all theories of "progress" and "modernity" as falacious, and believes that the nature of man's inner being is immutable, it again becomes evident that this book of poems has little to do with the historical reality of a city called Buenos Aires in the year 1923. Instead, one of the principal purposes of the book is to "refute" time; indeed, time is the work's main protagonist. Time is seen as the only constant factor in man's life: time is a stability in man's life because it is predictable; like the river, it is forever flowing and forever the same. The poet knows that time eventually destroys man and all the things that are dear to him, but simultaneously it is the very substance of man's being. *Fervor de Buenos Aires* is a search for the meaning of, or the justification for, mortal man's existence; the poet can find no facile solutions—if all men must die, what can the ultimate purpose of existence be? The poet is worried about being reduced to total oblivion. Heroes and dictators are forgotten; their memories are reduced to dust. All that is left of his own ancestors are a few old pieces of furniture, a handful of personal trinkets, and some fading daguerreotypes. The poetic voice of *Fervor de Buenos Aires* does not want to be reduced to utter nothingness; it aspires to live on in the consciousness of future readers. The poetry itself becomes both a weapon to check time's flow and a vehicle through which the poet can attain at least a small measure of immortality. *Fervor de Buenos Aires* is the key to the rest of Borges' work—in it can be found the genesis of his later poetry and the thematic material for most of his short stories. Borges himself agrees with this assessment:

> And yet, looking back on it now, I think I have never strayed beyond that book. I feel that all my subsequent writing has only developed themes first taken up there; I feel that all during my lifetime I have been rewriting that one book (AE p. 225).

Notes

[1] Jorge Luis Borges, "An Autobiographical Essay," *The Aleph and Other Stories 1933–1969*, Norman Thomas di Giovanni, editor and translator (New York: E.P. Dutton, 1978), p. 223–224. Hereafter cited in text as AE.

[2] Emir Rodríguez Monegal, *Jorge Luis Borges: A Literary Biography* (New York: E.P. Dutton, 1978), p. 173. Hereafter cited in text as RM.

[3] Guillermo de Torre, *Ultraísmo, existencialismo, y objetivismo en literatura* (Madrid: Ediciones Guadarrama, 1968), p. 116. Hereafter cited in text as DT.

[4] Enrique Díez-Canedo, "Fervor de Buenos Aires," *Jorge Luis Borges: El escritor y la crítica*, Jaime Alazraki, editor (Madrid: Taurus Ediciones, 1976), p. 21–22.

[5] Jorge Luis Borges, *Obra poética 1923–1969* (Madrid: Alianza Editorial, 1972), p. 9.

[6] Jorge Luis Borges, *Selected Poems 1923–1967*, ed. Norman Thomas di Giovanni (New York: Dell Publishing Co., 1969), p. 282. This work contains good documentation of the many revisions found in successive editions of Borges' poetry; see p. 281–328. Hereafter cited in text as SP.

[7] Carlos Meneses, *Poesía juvenil de Jorge Luis Borges* (Barcelona: Editor José J. de Olañeta, 1978), p. 15.

[8] Roland Barthes, *Writing Degree Zero*, trans. A. Lavers and C. Smith (New York: Hill and Wang, 1968), p. 10–11. Hereafter cited in text as RB.

[9] Jorge Luis Borges, *Obra poética 1923–1964* (Buenos Aires: Emecé Editores, S.A., 1964), p. 17. Hereafter cited in text as OP.

[10] Jorge Luis Borges, *Otras inquisiciones* (Buenos Aires: Emecé Editores, 1960), p. 256.

4

Moon Across the Way

Upon returning to Buenos Aires in 1924 from his second European sojourn, Borges plunged back into the city's literary life. He became involved with the literary set surrounding the magazine *Martín Fierro* (whose first issue appeared in February 1924 and which ceased publication in 1927) and eventually contributed some twenty-two pieces to the pages of that magazine, including three poems, a dozen articles, and seven reviews. Nowadays, Borges prefers to disassociate himself as much as possible from this group and its many literary and political sins:

> I disliked what *Martín Fierro* stood for, which was the French idea that literature is being continually renewed—that Adam is reborn every morning, and also for the idea that, since Paris had literary cliques that wallowed in publicity and bickering, we should be up to date and do the same. One result of this was that a sham literary feud was cooked up in Buenos Aires—that between Florida and Boedo.[1]

"Florida" referred to the downtown business district and symbolized more establishment-oriented, conservative views, and the concept of art for art's sake, whereas "Boedo"—a proletarian neighborhood—represented a more radical, engagé view of literature. To his chagrin, Borges was placed in the Florida group due to his bourgeois, upper-middle-class family ties and his nonpolitical view of literature:

> I'd have preferred to be in the Boedo group, since I was writing about the old Northside and slums, sadness, and sunsets. But I was informed by one of the two conspirators—they were Ernesto Palacio, of Florida, and Roberto Mariani, of Boedo—that I was already one of the Florida warriors and that it was too late for me to change. The whole thing was

> a put-up job. Some writers belonged to both groups—Roberto Arlt and Nicolás Olivari, for example. This sham is now taken into serious consideration by "credulous universities." But it was partly publicity, partly a boyish prank. (AE p. 236)

Some members of the Boedo group were members of the nascent Argentine communist party and hoped to use the feud as a way to liquidate the avant-garde movement and promote socialist realism in its place. Despite some of these political overtones, there clearly were a lot of pranks and plain old fun connected with the Florida-Boedo polemics, and Borges' current disclaimers cannot mask the fact that he derived a good deal of enjoyment from the *Martín Fierro*'s numerous literary gatherings and banquets (the publication of *Luna de enfrente* was feted at one of those banquets). However, as Rodríguez Monegal points out, Borges usually published lighter-weight, more journalistic pieces in the pages of *Martín Fierro*, while saving more heavyweight, serious material for his own magazine, the second *Proa* (which he founded in August, 1924, with Ricardo Güiraldes and others; it continued publishing until January 1926). Borges wrote seventeen articles and three reviews for the second *Proa* besides using its pages to début several poems later to be published in *Luna de enfrente*. Both Güiraldes and Borges used *Proa*'s publishing arm to get new books into print: Güiraldes used this forum to launch *Don Segundo Sombra* while Borges published *Luna de enfrente*.

Rodríguez Monegal concisely summarizes the content of much of Borges' literary activity at that time:

> Both in his poetry and in his more important articles he attempted to capture the essence of a certain Argentine tone of voice, a form of the national identity that had been ignored by those who wanted the country to be progressive and modern. On the contrary, he found the real Argentina in gaucho poetry and in the humble outskirts of Buenos Aires. But he also rejected the folklorists' reactionary attempt to re-create a dead past. His recovery of the past was done by intuition and feeling, by an imaginative projection into an extra dimension of time.[2]

This is clearly a very different Borges from the one evidenced during the heady ultraist days in Madrid just a few years before. This search for the lost essences of the Argentine past stands in stark contrast to his former avant-garde pan-humanism, best exemplified by his fascination with the German expressionists. Instead of striving to be international Borges now filled the work of this period with Argentinisms in an attempt to be as Argentine as possible. In retrospect, it can also be seen as a device to put even more distance between himself and the avant-garde movements in Europe and in Latin America in order to enable him to forge his own more personal style divorced from contemporary literary movements and "schools." The most obvious avant-garde elements that appear in *Luna de enfrente* are superficial in nature; an example is his phonetic spelling: he substituted "j" for "g." With the passage of time, Borges regretted these youthful excesses and suppressed most of the phonetic spelling and substituted standard Spanish words for most of the Argentinisms in later additions of his work. Speaking humorously of his abuse of Argentinisms in one of his essay collections published in the 1920's, Borges states that:

> ... I tried to be as Argentine as I could. I got hold of Segovia's dictionary of Argentinisms and worked in so many local words that many of my countrymen could hardly understand it. Since I have mislaid the dictionary, I'm not sure I would any longer understand the book myself, and so have given it up as utterly hopeless. (AE p. 231)

Evaluating his 1925 poetry collection Borges states:

> Of the poems of this time, I should perhaps have also suppressed my second collection, *Luna de enfrente* (Moon Across the Way). It was published in 1925 and is a kind of riot of sham local color. Among its tomfooleries were the spelling of my first name in the nineteenth-century Chilean fashion as "Jorje" (it was a halfhearted attempt at phonetic spelling); the spelling of the Spanish for "and" as "i" instead of "y" (our greatest writer, Sarmiento, had done the same, trying to be as un-Spanish as he could); and the omission of the final "d" in words like "autoridá" and "ciudá." In later editions, I dropped the worst poems, pruned the eccentricities, and, successively—through several reprintings—revised and toned down the verses. (AE p. 232)

Luna de enfrente first appeared in 1925 with a preface and twenty-seven poems. It was spruced up with five of Norah Borges' woodcuts, and three hundred copies were printed; this has become Borges' scarcest book. When *Luna de enfrente* reappeared as part of *Poemas* (1943) the preface and eight poems were deleted. *All* of the remaining poems were revised to some degree: seven received minor touch-ups, eight got moderate revisions and four were extensively overhauled. Borges also added two new poems to the collection: "Al coronel Francisco Borges" and "Manuscrito hallado en un libro de Joseph Conrad." In addition, Borges began the process of eliminating typographical quirks by no longer printing the poem titles all in lower case letters or using "i" instead of "y" for the Spanish word "and." The 1953 edition of *Poemas* shows relatively few changes in *Luna de enfrente*: five poems were given minor revisions while the rest appeared as they did in 1943. The 1958 edition of *Poemas* reprinted twelve of the poems identically from the 1953 printing (except for typographical errors of which there were many); eight poems received minor changes and one poem—"Jactancia de quietud"—received moderate revisions. *Obra poética* appeared in 1964 and showed a further refining of *Luna de enfrente*: only four poems appeared as in their 1958 printing, six received minor revisions, eight got moderate revisions, and two—"Los llanos" and "A Rafael Cansinos Asséns"—were extensively revised. The 1966 and 1967 editions of *Obra poética* reproduce identically *Luna de enfrente*'s 1964 version except for the fact that the 1967 edition deleted two poems—"A Rafael Cansinos Asséns" and "Al Coronel Francisco Borges." As in the case of *Fervor de Buenos Aires*, *Luna de enfrente* received its biggest overhaul in 1969 when the Emecé publishing company came out with new editions of Borges' previous poetry. Starting with the 1967 printing, Borges deleted one more poem from *Luna de enfrente* (leaving a total of only eighteen) and reprinted only two poems identically. Of the remaining sixteen works, four escaped with minor revisions, five received moderate revisions, six got extensive revisions, and one poem was totally rewritten.[3]

Martin Stabb describes the content of *Luna de enfrente* as a collection of poems of "intimacy" and "personal involvement," pointing to the personification of inanimate objects such as the city streets and the pampa, the use of the familiar "tú" form or the first person "yo" form in many of the poems, and to the presence of several love poems. The sunsets and twilight that undermined and softened objective reality in *Fervor de Buenos Aires* are also present in *Luna de enfrente*. Time again surfaces as a main protagonist in the poems; however, the emphasis is more on exploring the relationship between time and memory, and less on halting the flow of time. Memory is the atemporal space in which time's flow can be checked by converting the past into the eternal present of recollection. Memory protects past experience from being totally destroyed by time's passage.

Another theme that surfaces in *Luna de enfrente* is a deep feeling of world weariness on the part of the poetic persona who feels that he has done and experienced it all already, and that there is nothing new for him to do or say. Commenting on this theme, Stabb asks the following rhetorical question:

> Is Borges retreating from life or is he simply stating what has become a cornerstone of his esthetic edifice: that there is nothing new under the sun; that changes, progress, novelty and history are simply a reshuffling of a limited number of pre-existing elements?[4]

Clearly both of these aspects are present in *Fervor de Buenos Aires* and *Luna de enfrente*; the poetic persona desires to create an inner, private, personal space that is out of the mainstream of contemporary life and out of the swift current of time's flow. Once the possibility of real "change," "progress," and "novelty" have been denied, all political, religious, and social dogmas become meaningless. Confronted with an external world governed by invalid ideologies, to maintain its integrity the poet has no other recourse but to create his own interior, intellectual and emotional world which then becomes more "real" for the poet than objective reality which is truly "false" for having been based on a series of falacious original premises.

Borges summarizes the content of *Luna de enfrente* in his preface to the original 1925 edition:

> This book is a token of my poverty, written not in passion but in meditation. In these pages the reader will find a long, weary street out in the western stretches of town, sad in the sunset, and the loneliness of love denied. (SP p. 270)

Also in this preface, Borges states that he sees our daily lives as a dialogue between life and death "woven of memories." The poet stresses his sincerity; he feels that each poet in order to be genuine must express the things that come naturally to him: "Let every poet praise the things that are akin to himself, for that is real poetry. I have celebrated those things akin to me, those things I deeply feel" (SP p. 270). Borges goes on to state that he has little interest in discussions of technique; any form will do "as long as rhyme is unobtrusive." He admits to using the street slang of Buenos Aires in the poems as well as using a more standard Spanish. Finally he explains the title of the book—*Moon Across the Way*. The moon is a symbol of poetry, "the across the way does not change this but makes it into a city moon, brings it nearer, turning it into a Buenos Aires moon, everyone's moon. This is the way I like it, and this is the way I see it from the street" (SP p. 270). The "street" poems make up the largest thematic group in *Luna de enfrente*. The first poem of the collection—"Calle con almacén rosado"—fits into this category and also serves as the "hello" or introductory poem just as the poem "Las calles" did in *Fervor de Buenos Aires*. "Calle con almacén rosado" has for its setting the city streets in the moments before dawn when the stars are disappearing; it is a magical moment, ripe for thought and fantasy. The poet has spent the night wandering through the streets; the dawn is viewed as a symbol of the fear of doing new things and the night's uneasiness in the pre-dawn hours ("inquietud") is really his own. He winds up by chance on a particular street corner; again, the pampa's emptiness can be felt as a presence beyond the city's edge. Just a few scant elements paint the scene: some weed-covered empty lots and the pink store on the corner. The store appears like a glowing ember that conceived the dawn, and the whole corner seems familiar like a memory—yet another reminder that memory has more substance than reality. The poet is happy to affirm the street's existence with his presence; the poem is a hymn of praise to these humble streets which he feels more deeply than the land or sea:

> no he mirado los ríos ni la mar ni la sierra,
> pero intimó conmigo la luz de Buenos Aires[5]

Clearly the poet sees the streets as repositories of peace, stability, protection—a place to be accepted without question. The last two lines of the poem sum up this feeling and round out this "street invocation":

> Calle grande y sufrida,
> eres la única música de que sabe mi vida. (OP p. 72)

The next street poem—"Al horizonte de un suburbio"—is really a hymn to the grandeur of the pampa. However, it is a view of the pampa as the poet prefers to see it—glimpsed from the security of the city's outermost suburbs. In the poem, the poet identifies with the pampa and feels one with it; the pampa is "good" and "unchanging," its stability is like a religious ritual such as the prayer "Avemaría." The repetition of the word "pampa" before each stanza gives the poem a formal, serious tone much like a prayer litany. The poem is dominated by violent imagery: the long-suffering pampa is violated by the rude invasion of the city streets. Nonetheless, by its permanence, the pampa has a spiritual or god-like quality which the poet has internalized in a mystical communion:

> Pampa sufrida y macha que estás en los cielos,
> no sé si eres la muerte. Sé que estás en mi pecho. (OP p. 74)

A poor neighborhood near the western edge of Buenos Aires and the La Chacarita cemetery is the setting for "Ultimo sol en Villa Ortúzar." The poet is awe-struck at the beauty of the sunset in these outskirts of town; violent, apocalyptical Christian imagery fills the poem; an angel, blood, and fire all contribute to this last-judgment vision of the setting sun. Indeed, these twilight moments are a time for visions since objective reality has been temporarily surpressed: "El mundo está como inservible y tirado" (OP p. 99). While the sky is still light, darkness has begun to collect in low places; the remaining light is concentrated in blue walls and in a noisy bunch of girls. The poet cannot tell whether one looming object is a tree or a god. The poet is overwhelmed by having so many worlds revealed to him simultaneously; countryside, sky, and suburbs are perceived in fresh, exciting ways. He feels momentarily rich with these twilight visions but realizes that he will soon return to the "poverty" of reality.

The poem "Montevideo," besides being a hymn of praise of Buenos Aires' smaller sister city across the River Plate, demonstrates how memory can preserve the past in an eternalized present. Montevideo—symbolizing a quiet, protected, sheltered, stable space—preserves the former atmosphere of Buenos Aires in present time; it is the persistence of Buenos Aires' past in the present. In this friendly, peaceful spot even the city's stones exude tenderness; and even the morning's sun appears sooner than in Buenos Aires, where dawn's light must be filtered through Montevideo to the east. This fine poem is marred only by a fireworks-display of typically ultraist imagery given in the first three lines, which could have been omitted with no detriment to the overall effect. The poet's attitude toward Montevideo is summed up in the last two verses:

> Ciudad que se oye como un verso.
> Calles con luz de patio. (OP p. 84)

Soothing poetry and the protected space of the patio symbolize Montevideo.

To seek a promise of immortality from the personified streets is the purpose of "Para una calle del oeste":

> Sé habrás de concederme inmortalidad, calle agreste.
> Eres ya sombra de mi vida. (OP p. 100)

From a technical standpoint, the personification of the street is strongly supported by a reversing of roles in the street-pedestrian relationship; it is the street that crosses the poet's nights with a straight, firm step. The poet is cognizant of the fact that he is mortal and that upon his death someone will "usurp" his evening strolls and his devotion to the streets and their accompanying stars. Nonetheless, there is hope in this process, for this person will have the same feelings and express the same wishes and longings to the street's skies as the poet himself would have expressed: "Yo resurgiré en su venidero asombro de ser" (OP p. 100). Here again, the city streets serve as a springboard to the world of the poet's personal metaphysics: individual men may die without leaving a trace but this is less tragic because in the continuing cycle of human existence, other men will do and feel the same things, thus providing a measure of immortality for those who have previously lived the same experiences. The poem is a reiteration of the theme of one man's representing all men that is so common in Borges' work as a whole.

Three of *Luna de enfrente*'s poems are direct autobiographical references that deal with the poet's second trip to Europe. The first of these—"A Rafael Cansinos Asséns"—is a personal, moving, warm tribute to his Madrid mentor and valued friend. The poem describes their last encounter—an evening walk in the old section of Madrid near the viaduct, savouring the pleasure of the night air and the throbbing stars above. The poet sees time as one of the culprits in this forced separation:

> Es trágica la entraña del adiós
> como de todo acontecer en que es notorio el Tiempo. (OP p. 86)

Although their separation could not be more complete—different time zones, seasons of the year, and even different stars in the heavens—a spiritual bond will always unite them. In this confessional tone, the genuine outpouring of human warmth so evident in this poem is proof that Borges' work is not always cold and intellectual.

"Singladura" is a product of the return sea voyage to Buenos Aires in 1924; the poet is enjoying a quiet late afternoon with his sister Norah on the deck of the transatlantic liner. He is awed by the vastness of the sea and its infinite qualities. The sea represents solitude and speaks of mysteries in its own indecipherable language; the sea is lasting—its monotony successfully resists the onslaught of time. The poet delights in discovering new perspectives on nature—the clouds, sunsets, and moonlight. The same moonlight he left under a stone archway in Spain is now tangled in the superstructure of the ship, and will be soon bathing a grove of willows in his homeland.

"La promisión en alta mar" is another poem composed aboard ship; the poet's first glimpses of the southern hemisphere's stars make him feel close to home despite the long distance left to be traveled. The poet expresses a clear desire to be back in his own familiar space—the streets of Buenos Aires—and there is a longing for the security and stability represented by the patio and its fountain. In addition to being symbols of all that is dear to him in his homeland—now sorely missed—the stars also represent the persistence of the physical elements of the universe as opposed to the fleeting quality of men's lives; they are constants in what is for the poet a disturbingly mutating world. Above all, the poem again expresses the poet's recognition that Buenos Aires is his destiny; it is the space in which he is most contented and which will weave the fiber of his daily existence.

There are several love poems in *Luna de enfrente*; one of the finest in Borges' entire erotic repetoire is "Amorosa anticipación" (entitled "Antelación de amor" in the original 1925 edition). In the poem, the poet holds the loved one in his arms as she sleeps; he now sees this person in a new, mysterious light. She radiates pureness and innocence in a manner that he had never observed before; she is "quieta y resplandeciente como una dicha en la / selección del recuerdo" (OP p. 77). The poet feels god-like in this situation; he has penetrated into the deepest recesses of another person's being and has enjoyed a special perspective that the person herself can never see or share. There is a timeless quality to this poem in which the glow of this unique moment is preserved in the eternity of archetype or myth.

Another fine love poem is "Dualidá en una despedida" (entitled "Una despedida" in the most recent editions). The poet focuses on the particular afternoon in which he was forced to say good-by to his love. There is a brief burst of apocalyptical Christian imagery in the form of a menacing "dark angel." This is quickly followed by the erotic aspect of this parting: "Tarde cuando vivieron nuestros labios en la desnuda y triste intimidá de los besos" (OP p. 78). The couple is doubly united by their suffering, whose cause again can be traced to time:

>El tiempo inevitable se desbordaba
>sobre el inútil tajamar del abrazo. (OP p. 78)

Time puts an end to the afternoon's embraces by bringing on the night, and the reality of parting imposes itself. The poet leaves with dual feelings—an exhilaration at this wonderfully sensual afternoon that he has spent with his love, tinged with the pain of separation. Among all afternoons, this special one remains vivid like a dream in the poet's memory (again dreams appear as superior "realities"). The poet's separate life goes on but his longing for the absent loved person increases and becomes more ardent with the passage of time.

"Casas como ángeles" is a fantasy love poem. Blue houses at a certain street intersection have a special glow at twilight that conjures up adventurous visions in the poet's mind. In this erotic fantasy, he sees himself entering one of the houses to find a beautiful young woman already awaiting his arrival in the living room. He sees her pale arms shining in the dim light, and her dark hair; he stares into her deep eyes. The poet is clearly expressing his desire for passion, his need to be wanted, to be loved. Unfortunately, it is equally clear that frustration in the reality of love is the source of such fantasies.

There are two "mood poems" in *Luna de enfrente*; these are

poems whose sole reason for being is to create an intense atmosphere, usually exotic or mysterious. Thus, the poem "Benarés" in *Fervor de Buenos Aires* finds its counterpart in *Luna de enfrente*. In "Dakar" the poet tries to penetrate the mysterious realm of the exotic lure of Africa—a continent full of "hazañas, ídolos, reinos, arduos bosques y espadas" (OP p. 91). The focus is on three hostile natural elements—sun, desert, and sea—that openly challenge man in the African environment. His "painting" is completed with just a few brush strokes: the blue robe of a chieftain, a glowing mosque, the sun scaling the city's walls. The poet has full realization of the incompleteness of his vision and the limitations of his poem; in the last line he confesses that of all that Africa symbolizes: "Yo he logrado un atardecer y una aldea" (OP p. 91). The other atmosphere poem is "Manuscrito hallado en un libro de Joseph Conrad." The poem has been interpreted in a more serious vein by critics such as María Adela Renard:

> El contacto directo con la naturaleza ofrece al hombre la posibilidad de meditar sobre sus eternos dilemas existenciales, llevándolo a tomar distancia respecto del universo. Paradójicamente, es una manera de tenerlo más cerca y comprender su sentido.[6]

It appears, however, that the poem has less profound origins; it was born out of a practical joke played on Borges by his friend Néstor Ibarra who commissioned the poem for a fee (which Borges actually was paid). The poem was supposed to be used to advertise some tobacco product and Borges agreed to write the poem only under the condition that he not be required to actually name the product in the text. The title gives a clue to the type of atmosphere that the poet wishes to evoke—a stifling tropical atmosphere reminiscent of *Lord Jim*. The first of the three stanzas is full of intense heat and blinding sunlight. The second stanza is a night river scene in which a man appears lying in a canoe leisurely smoking while lazily staring into the starry heavens. In the final stanza, the tobacco smoke wafts across the constellations while all care and sense of time and place fade away. A less esoteric interpretation of the poem might be: smoke our brand to relax and to forget all of your troubles. However, the last lines do suggest multiple levels of interpretation: they represent a return to a primeval world, a return to the original essence of things and to the glorious freshness of the first moments of creation.

Among the several historical poems in *Luna de enfrente* is "Dulcia linquimos arva."[7] It is a nostalgic poem that conjures up an idealized vision of the pioneer days in Argentine history in which the pampa was tamed and settled. References to Borges' own ancestors (his maternal grandfather and great-grandfather and paternal grandfather) form the framework upon which the poem is constructed.[8] In this nostalgic vision, these early settlers had special links with the natural elements that surrounded them—earth, fire, water, air—and lived in harmony with them. There was a certain purity and pristine quality to their existence. Their lives had regular rhythms that lent themselves to the establishment of stability and order:

> Su jornada fue clara como un río
> y era fresca su tarde como el aljibe del patio
> y en su vivir eran las cuatro estaciones
> como los cuatro versos de una copla esperada. (OP p. 93)

In addition, although these pioneers were worldly and lived through many adventures, their lives were somehow less complicated; the universe was perceived in clearer, much simpler terms: "se sintieron confesos en el canto de un pájaro" (OP p. 94). Healthy living and clear consciences defined their existence:

> resplandecientes y altos eran sus días
> hechos de cielo y llano. (OP p. 94)

In the last four lines the poet confesses that in contrast to his ancestors, he is a city dweller and has lost contact with the land and other elements of nature in their purest state. He is clearly saddened by the poverty of this change in life style, and modern "improvements" such as the streetcar only serve to remind him of this deterioration in the quality of life as he perceives it. Moreover, it is equally clear that the poet is not happy with the slot of historical time in which he has been forced to live his life—he clearly expresses a desire to have lived in another era and to have played a different role (an active, adventurous one) in society.

The poem "Al Coronel Francisco Borges" is another historical poem which draws its raw material from Jorge Luis' family pantheon. Here again we see a fascination with men of action, but it is tempered with the down-to-earth realization of the irreality and futility of all "heroism." This message of the ultimate failure of heroism comes over much more directly in this poem than in "Inscripción sepulcral" from *Fervor de Buenos Aires* in which the protagonist was Borges' maternal great-grandfather. The hero—in this case, Francisco Borges—had no control over his life. The battles and events dragged him onward relentlessly and uncontrollably; in such a context bravery is useless because the outcome is preordained:

> Porque eso fue tu vida:
> Una cosa que arrastran las batallas.
>
> * * *
>
> El honor, la tristeza, la soledad
> y el inútil coraje. (OP p. 85)

The central section of the poem is an ennumeration of the elements that made up the Coronel's life. However, fate—in the form of a violent death—stalked the Coronel, and all of the events in his life were a mere prelude to this one inescapable moment. The Coronel realizes this, wraps himself in a white poncho and mounts a fine steed to confront his inevitable fate. Implicit in the last line ("morías con dos balas en el estómago" [OP p. 85]) is an emphatic rhetorical question: ¿y qué? (for what?).

"Los llanos" is one of the two historical poems in *Luna de enfrente* dealing with the life of Juan Facundo Quiroga who (along with the dictator Rosas) represents for Borges the quintessence of the anti-heroic man of action. Quiroga's empire was built on violence, blood, and death which is reflected in the imagery of knives, flames, and sex. The poem is masterfully constructed: its chief artifice is the skillful use of repetition to create a gradually accelerating rhythm that starts slowly with the repetition of the word "imperio" and reaches a frenzied speed with the maddening repetition of the conjunction "y." The frenzied rhythm comes to an abrupt halt with the last four lines:

> Todo ello se perdió como el tumulto de un
> / poniente se pierde.
> Es triste que el recuerdo encierre todo
> y más aún si es bochornoso el recuerdo. (OP p. 76)

All of this long list of activities that characterized Facundo's career—although now gone forever—is recorded in the memory of the plains, thus contributing to their tiredness. Memory is like an archive that stores everything, the good and the bad; this explains the plain's fatigue in preserving this endless catalogue of events. Borges explores this theme again in one of his short stories, "Funes el Memorioso," written many years later. One also can see a projection of the poet's own interior emotional state in lines such as "La llanura es una estéril copia del alma" (OP p. 75). Like the plains he describes, the poet feels old and tired; his soul is stricken with a low-grade but persistent pain—the pain of memory. Implicit is the wish that some of the plain's memories and some of his own could somehow be erased forever.

One of the finest poems in *Luna de enfrente* is another historical poem dealing with Juan Facundo Quiroga: "El general Quiroga va en coche al muere."[9] The poem—one of the few in *Luna de enfrente* with a more traditional structure—is divided into seven quatrains characterized by considerable assonance. The first quatrain creates a mysterious, bleak, unearthly atmosphere—an almost lunar landscape—that sets the tone for the rest of the work and helps prepare the reader for the jump to a mythical space at the end of the poem. The second quatrain presents the general's coach (whose bouncing rhythm can be actually felt in the verses) and the four black horses pulling it, which clearly symbolize death:

> Cuatro tapaos con pinta de muerte en la negrura
> tironeaban seis miedos y un valor desvelado. (OP p. 80)

Quiroga's death is not supposed to be a surprise to the reader; knowledge of the conclusion helps to build the mood of tension and suspense. The third quatrain reminds the reader of the historical events that the poem relates—the violent death of Quiroga and his escort. "How vain to go to death in a carriage!" exclaims the poet. The fourth and fifth quatrains take place in the protagonist Quiroga's mind—he is proud, self-confident and defiant:

> Aquí estoy afianzado y metido en la vida
> como la estaca pampa bien metida en la pampa. (OP p. 80)

Quiroga's challenge to fate is answered in the sixth quatrain narrated by the poet: the dawn reveals the dead "caudillo." The seventh quatrain carries the reader to a mythical plain ("Ya muerto, ya de pie, ya inmortal, ya fantasma" [OP p. 81]) in which the dead Quiroga—standing, immortal, a ghost—is condemned to the hell he so justly deserves, but where he still cruelly commands over the tortured souls of the men and animals that died with him. Paradoxically, the anti-hero is more "alive" now that he is dead: Quiroga lives on in the eternal present of myth by force of his extreme infamy. Martin Stabb provides some insight into why Borges wrote historical poems of this nature:

> In "El General Quiroga va en coche al muere" Borges provides an insight into the kind of historical characters and events which were to dominate much of his later work, especially his prose. What fascinates him are those moments in which an individual—soldier, bandit, or similar man of action—reaches a crucial point in his life: the dramatic junctures where a turn of fate, a sudden decision, or a dazzling revelation cause a man to follow one path or another. Such events are

delicate points of balance which determine whether a man shall become a hero or traitor, a martyr or coward.[10]

The final thematic group to be studied in *Luna de enfrente* are the "philosophical poems" in which the poet reveals elements of his personal value system; some of these poems can be even more accurately described as poems of self-justification.

"Jactancia de quietud" reveals the poet's sensitivity to peer criticism of his work: clearly poems like the ones in *Luna de enfrente* would please neither the "Boedo" group (due to their lack of preoccupation with current social problems), nor the "Florida" brethren of ultraist tendencies. Here, Borges repeats in poetry what he stated in prose in the preface to the work: each poet must write what comes most naturally to him. The first three lines of "Jactancia de quietud" mock writers (like the poet's own critics) who pour forth showy displays of "wisdom" to dispel the darkness of ignorance. Meanwhile, the poet knows who he is, understands his limits but tries with only partial success to understand the ambitious writers he has just described:

> Seguro de mi vida y de mi muerte, miro los
> ambiciosos y quisiera entenderlos. (OP p. 82)

The poet's critics are active and combative; they speak in platitudes of "humanity" and the "fatherland." The poet's humanity is the brotherhood of all men and his only "fatherland" is made up of his own family circle, memories, his poetry, and his inner emotional being. The poet steadfastly refuses to participate in the world of the greedy: they are "unique" and "indispensable" while he is content to remain someone or anyone. While others write for the pleasure of hearing the praise of others, he writes only what he sincerely feels; lasting beauty is secondary to spiritual certainty:

> Yo solicito de mi verso que no me contradiga, y es mucho.
> Que no sea persistencia de hermosura, pero sí de certeza espiritual.
> (OP p. 83)

The poet wants solitude and the city streets to bear witness to his work; he does not need the approval of other men. Sure of himself and the path he has chosen, the poet weaves his existence with a slow step like one who has undertaken such a long journey that he never fully expects to arrive. His work will always be perfectible, incomplete: there are no attainable absolutes for mortal men.

"Casi juicio final" is a poem of self-affirmation; the poet affirms his worth, his purpose in life. In his wanderings through the city streets at night doing nothing (but thinking) he justifies his activities and gives himself needed praise. He recites a list of his accomplishments: he has borne witness to the world and its wonders, he has talked of eternal things (love, the universe), he has "sanctified" his city with verse, he has honored his ancestors (both biological and spiritual) with poetry. He believes that his work is superior to that of his detractors:

> He dicho asombro de vivir, donde otros dicen solamente costumbre.
> (OP p. 95)

He again affirms his existence with the cry: "He sido y soy." The poet's greatest accomplishment is that he has succeeded in forging emotions—that would otherwise have been forever lost—into lasting poetic capsules. Nonetheless, dark thoughts surge forth into his consciousness—that somehow he has not lived up to his promise, that he has failed—but he is strengthened and comforted by the moonlight. Finally, the poet poses the rhetorical question: how can mere men condemn him if the forces of the universe generously forgive all? This theme of his own personal unfulfilled promise is also the theme of the poem "Por los viales de Nimes," which Borges chose never to republish in subsequent editions of his poetry. In "Casi juicio final" Borges makes a subtle but significant change in a short phrase used by Garcilaso de la Vega; He changes "dolorido sentir" to "pensativo sentir": it is the successful union of form, intellectual content, and pure emotion that defines the essence of the poet's art.

"Mi vida entera" is an ennumeration of all of the things the poet has done so far: he has experienced happiness and sadness, travelled, met new people, fallen in love, tried to write, and seen many sunsets on the edge of Buenos Aires. The poem begins with an expression of the poet's genuine humility; he states that he is "único y semejante a vosotros." He continues: "Soy esa torpe intensidad que es un alma" (OP p. 98). The basic mood that the poem communicates is a weary feeling on the part of the poet who believes that he has already done and seen it all, and that there is nothing new that can happen to him. (The implied question is: "Is that all there is?") As part of an endless ritual he is repeating what others have already done, are now doing, and will continue to do in the future:

> Creo profundamente que eso es todo y que ni veré ni ejecutaré cosas nuevas.
> Creo que mis jornadas y mis noches se igualan en pobreza y en riqueza a las de Dios y a las de todos los hombres. (OP p. 98)

The repetition of Borges' theme of one man's being all men is very evident here along with an existential probing for a possible meaning to human existence.

"Versos de catorce" is *Luna de enfrente*'s "farewell" poem just as "Despedida" served a similar function in *Fervor de Buenos Aires*; the poem closes out this cycle of the poet's work. It is a multi-function poem: it is a hymn of praise to Buenos Aires, it expresses the poet's joy in returning home after his trip abroad, it lists the things he has written about in his work, and shows a recognition of his limitations. The poem also has another function not so directly stated: it serves as concrete proof to his critics that he is capable of using more traditional forms, and to prove that if he had previously used free verse, it was because he preferred it, not because he was incapable of writing anything else. In case the readers failed to notice the fourteen-syllable verses arranged in neat quatrains with obvious assonance, the poet used the title—"Fourteen-syllable verses"—to serve as an extra reminder. The repetition of the conjunction "y" makes it all flow together in yet another litany that justifies the poet's existence. The last two lines sum up the reason he wrote *Luna de enfrente*:

> Así voy devolviéndole a Dios unos centavos
> del caudal infinito que me pone en las manos. (OP p. 102)

The poet justifies his writing as an attempt to give back at least a little of the infinite abundance of riches given to him by the universe.

In summary, it is evident that *Luna de enfrente* reveals a poetic persona that is warm, sincere, sensitive, and loving; poems authentically expressing personal hopes, beliefs, fears, and love predominate. Rather than a cold, intellectual, and impersonal writer, *Luna de enfrente* reveals a determined poet who prefers to express his inner truths faithfully rather than to write for fame or for the approval of others.

Notes

[1] Jorge Luis Borges, "An Autobiographical Essay," *The Aleph and Other Stories 1933–1969*, Norman Thomas di Giovanni, editor and translator (New York: E.P. Dutton, 1978), p. 236. Hereafter cited in text as AE.

[2] Emir Rodríguez Monegal, *Jorge Luis Borges: A Literary Biography* (New York: E.P. Dutton, 1978), p. 191.

[3] Jorge Luis Borges, *Selected Poems 1923–1967*, ed. Norman Thomas di Giovanni (New York: Dell Publishing Co., 1969), p. 314–322. Di Giovanni carefully documents these mutations; his terminology has been used here: minor revisions affect one tenth or fewer lines, moderate revisions affect more than one tenth but fewer than one third of the lines and extensive revisions affect more than one third of the lines. Hereafter cited in text as SP.

[4] Martin S. Stabb, *Jorge Luis Borges* (Boston: Twayne Publishers, 1970), p. 41.

[5] Jorge Luis Borges, *Obra poética 1923–1964* (Buenos Aires: Emecé Editores, S.A., 1964), p. 72. Hereafter cited in text as OP.

[6] María Adela Renard, "Estudio preliminar," *Poesías: Jorge Luis Borges* (Buenos Aires: Editorial Kapelusz, S.A., 1977), p. 84.

[7] *Obra poética 1923–1964*, p. 93. The title is from Virgil, Eclogue I, line 3.

[8] *Obra poética 1923–1964*, p. 93. Borges speaks of Isidoro Suárez and Isidoro Acevedo in lines one and six. In line eighteen, the mention of the "gods" refers to the fact that Isidoro Suárez fought the Spaniards in the battle for Spanish American independence. In line nineteen, the reference is to Francisco Borges, Jorge Luis' paternal grandfather.

[9] *Obra poética 1923–1964*, p. 80–81. The term "al muere" means "a la muerte."

[10] Stabb, p. 42.

5

A San Martín Notebook

Borges' third Collection of poetry—*Cuaderno San Martín*—was published in 1929; in his "Autobiographical Essay," the poet gives his opinion of it:

> The third collection of the time, *Cuaderno San Martín* (the title has nothing to do with the national hero; it was merely the brand name of the out-of-fashion copybook into which I wrote the poems), includes some quite legitimate pieces, such as "La noche que en el Sur lo velaron," whose title has been strikingly translated by Robert Fitzgerald as "Deathwatch on the Southside," and "Muertes de Buenos Aires" (Deaths of Buenos Aires), about the two chief graveyards of the Argentine capital. One poem in the book (no favorite of mine) has somehow become a minor Argentine classic: "The Mythical Founding of Buenos Aires." This book, too, has been improved, or purified, by cuts and revisions down through the years.[1]

However, *Cuaderno San Martín* suffered fewer mutations than did *Fervor de Buenos Aires* and *Luna de enfrente*. In *Poemas (1922–1943)*, Borges deleted one poem, left one the same, gave minor revisions to eight and moderate revisions to one. *Poemas (1923–1953)* left four poems untouched, and gave minor revisions to six others. *Poemas (1923–1958)* reprinted five poems identically to the previous printing and gave minor revisions to the remaining five. In *Obra poética 1923–1964* four poems are left the same while six received minor touch-ups. *Obra poética 1923–1967* left nine texts the same and deleted one additional poem from the collection ("A la doctrina de pasión de tu voz"). Emecé's 1969 "reprint" of *Cuaderno San Martín* (published in a single volume along with *Luna de enfrente*) shows the most changes: only three poems were left the same, four received

107

minor revisions, and two received moderate revisions. As previously mentioned, one can see that *Cuaderno San Martín* was given less extensive overhauls than either *Fervor de Buenos Aires* or *Luna de enfrente*.

Cuaderno San Martín also proved to be a financial success: the poet won the second municipal prize for literature which carried with it a sizeable monetary stipend. Borges used part of the money to buy a secondhand set of the eleventh edition of the *Encyclopaedia Britannica*—encyclopedias had always fascinated him—and used the rest to help finance his biography of Evaristo Carriego (it was published in 1930 and proved to be a decided flop; Borges published a revised and improved version of the work in 1955).

Cuaderno San Martín is prefaced with a quote taken from a letter by Edward FitzGerald to Bernard Barton:

> As to an occasional copy of verses, there are few men who have leisure to read, and are possessed of any music in their souls, who are not capable of versifying on some ten or twelve occasions during their natural lives: at a proper conjunction of the stars. There is no harm in taking advantage of such occasions.[2]

This quote is similar to the "A quien leyere" that precedes *Fervor de Buenos Aires*; it expresses the same humility—the idea that writing good poetry is not some extraordinary act of genius of which few are capable, but rather it is an activity that can be successfully cultivated by the many. The quote also reinforces the poet's faith in the muse as a source of poetic inspiration along with the corollary idea that a good poet is never totally free to write whatever and whenever he pleases; instead, the poet writes what was meant for him to write given his particular slot in history. Again, this concept of the muse as being essential to the poetic process is not new; it is basically a restatement of what Borges wrote in his "Prólogo" to *Fervor de Buenos Aires*—the poet may have matured, but his basic esthetics have not radically changed.

Cuaderno San Martín's poems fall into two thematic groups—poems of nostalgia and poems dealing with death. Indeed, death is the book's obsession, whether it be the actual death of people or the figurative death of the old patterns of life in his most beloved neighborhoods.

"La fundación mítica de Buenos Aires" opens the collection and serves to create the world of the mythical eternal present in which Borges longs to preserve forever intact the Palermo neighborhood of his youth by playfully distorting history according to his personal whim. In the poem's last two lines, the poet confesses that he cannot even conceive of the idea that there was a time when Buenos Aires (and Palermo) did not exist:

> A mí se me hace cuento que empezó Buenos Aires
> La juzgo tan eterna como el agua y el aire. (OP p. 106)

Borges chose a more traditional form for this mock epic poem—quatrains with regularly occurring assonance. The first three quatrains recount the difficulties encountered by the early explorers and settlers of the region. The second quatrain holds just about the only morsel of humor in the entire collection by recounting how Juan Díaz "fasted" and the Indians ate—the Indians are said to have dined on the hapless sixteenth-century explorer. In the third quatrain, the poet prepares the reader for the fourth quatrain's leap into fantasy by populating the Atlantic Ocean with mythological sea creatures and magic stones that lure ships to disaster. The fourth quatrain begins with a vision of the insecure settlers living in small dwellings clinging to the coast; but, instead of recounting the standard historical tradition of the founding of the city near the "Boca" area (south of the modern downtown area), the poet has them living in his Palermo north-side neighborhood. In fact, it is the turn-of-the-twentieth-century Palermo that Borges describes here, complete with its pink general store on the corner with people playing cards in the back, and its "compadritos" or local hoods. In this eternal present of myth, the poet has his own block—the one he grew up on existing in all of its details—plopped down on the pampa in splendid isolation, oblivious to the fact that the other side of the street (and all the other streets of the city) did not yet even exist. Clearly, Borges is expressing his desire to find a way to preserve forever intact his childhood vision of the Palermo neighborhood, which explains his choice of a mythical space, which in turn gives free reign to fantasy. In addition, the poem can be seen as an example of Borges' nativism; the poet wants to create a glorious mythical past for Buenos Aires comparable to that of other great cities.

The one direct political reference (to Yrigoyen) in the poem—rare in Borges' work—is noteworthy. Although the Palermo described in this poem is the turn-of-the-century neighborhood that Borges grew up in—which would tend to favor the thesis that the political slogan on the wall referred to Yrigoyen's 1916 victorious presidential election campaign, it seems even more plausible that it refers to Yrigoyen's successful 1928 presidential bid which Borges openly supported (he was a political activist in the Committee of Young Intellectuals that was formed to support Yrigoyen). The insertion of this cocky wall slogan for Yrigoyen, even if not a direct propaganda plug for his candidate, clearly shows that politics and the 1928 presidential race were vivid in Borges' consciousness at the time *Cuaderno San Martín* was published. In short, although this one brief reference does not change Borges' basic belief that good literature should not get too deeply entwined in the world of politics, it does undermine the claims of those who complain of Borges' total political apathy.

"Elegía de los portones" is a eulogy of the Palermo that was then fast disappearing (today even the "portones" are long gone):

> Esta es una elegía
> de un Palermo pintado con vaivén de recuerdo
> y que se va en la muerte chica de los olvidos. (OP p. 107)

The several repetitions of the phrase "Esta es una elegía . . ." give the beginning of the poem a weighty, serious tone. The poet shows his affection by personifying the neighborhood using the characteristic Argentine "vos" ("Palermo desganado, vos tenías . . ."). The festive and suggestive night life is highlighted, along with stark contrasts—the quiet, protected patio and the neighborhood tough which Borges idealizes:

> Había cosas felices,
> cosas que sólo fueron para alegrar el alma:
> el arriate del patio
> y el andar hamacado del compadre. (OP p. 108)

Clearly, one of the old Palermo's virtues was that time passed more slowly there than in the hectic downtown area:

> El día era más largo en tus veredas
> que en las calles del Centro, (OP p. 108)

However, the poet realizes that these times are now past (note the use of the preterite tense—"fuiste"): "Yo digo que así fuiste en un día del tiempo" (OP p. 109). Now the poet wanders these same streets at night to recapture a glimpse of that special glow that Palermo once had; the pink corner buildings seem more pleasant to him than the clouds, and the neighborhood streets tame the sky making the atmosphere more peaceful than the outlying countryside. What Borges is clearly expressing in poems such as these is his desire to have actually been a colorful turn-of-the-century Palermo resident as was his much idealized hero Evaristo Carriego; the poet would have preferred to have been born in a different time slot, to have had a different temperament (that of a man of action like the "compadrito"), and to have enjoyed a life style that he now can only fantasize about. Borges' fascination with life in Palermo during this period is proven by his decision to devote his energies to writing a biography of Carriego soon after the completion of *Cuaderno San Martín*.

Whereas "Elegía de los portones" was Borges' elegy to the whole Palermo neighborhood, "Fluencia natural del recuerdo" is his elegy to the actual house that he grew up in there. The poem evokes the atmosphere of his family's Palermo home, focusing particularly on its garden with its palm tree, old mill, and well—all of which are true to life descriptions. The poet goes on to describe his childhood games and fantasies that were played out in that garden, and gives the reader a glimpse of the friendly general store on the corner that often provided the necessary props for those games. The last quatrain sums up the mood:

> Jardín, yo depondré mi oración
> para seguir siempre acordándome:
> buena voluntad de dar sombra
> fueron tus árboles. (OP p. 111)

The poet wants to preserve this holy place in the permanence of his memory; the Palermo house symbolized peace and protection—a sheltered, innocent life like that of the womb.

"Barrio norte" is still another nostalgic evocation of Buenos Aires' rapidly changing northern suburbs. The poet speaks of a secret—the neighborhood and how it used to be; it is a "poor" secret because it is kept not by mysteries or oaths but rather by indifference and mere forgetting:

> lo preserva el olvido, que es el modo más pobre del misterio.
>   (OP p. 127)

The neighborhood was once like a warm friendship but only a few scant traces of how it once was are left now, and this changed state of affairs is chilling to those who remember how it used to be: "Ese disperso amor es nuestro desanimado secreto" (OP p. 128). In addition, the poet is cognizant of the fact that his "secret" is shared by fewer and fewer people:

> Una cosa invisible está pereciendo del mundo,
> un amor no más ancho que una música. (OP p. 128)

Nonetheless, the poet persists in his tenacious loyalty to his beloved Palermo neighborhood, and sees echoes of the past preserved in the trees and in the reflected light of sunrises and sunsets—it is clearly a world tenuously maintained more by intuition and by an emotional presence than by objective reality.

The last poem in the collection—"El Paseo de Julio"—is related to the other neighborhood street poems only in its thematic raw material—the evocation of the atmosphere of a neighborhood. In this case the atmosphere created is that of a hell on earth. The poet describes a downtown honky-tonk night life area of the city in very disagreeable terms—which only serves to highlight and accentuate the tranquility projected by the Palermo poem series. The poem emphasizes the seamy side of life and serves as a strong denunciation of an ugly reality. The poet admits to being familiar with this part of the city, but claims never to have felt at home or at ease there. The poet probes the function of this neighborhood—its reason for being: "pero mi verso es de interrogación y de prueba" (OP p. 129). Strong pejorative terms predominate: mutilated, nightmare, ugliness, chaos. The poet also personifies this neighborhood, but with an accusing judgmental tone:

> Eres la perdición fraguándose un mundo
> con los reflejos y las deformaciones de éste; (OP p. 130)

It is a commercial world of prostitution and drunken brawls: it is dehumanizing. The irony here of course is that many of these same denounced activities were rampant in the poet's idealized Palermo world; however, somehow in Palermo the human contacts were more personalized, more genuine. Downtown, the same acts have become mechanical, depersonalized, false, and just plain nasty and dirty; the Paseo de Julio's worst sin is its stress on the present, the here and now, the current fashion and way of doing things: this in itself is worthy of condemnation. The poet asks for this detestable neighborhood to justify itself:

> pero, ¿qué dios, que ídolo, qué veneración la tuya,
> Paseo de Julio?

The poet does not wait for the street's reply to his rhetorical question and moves directly instead to the stinging finale:

> Tu vida pacta con la muerte;
> toda felicidad, con sólo existir, te es adversa. (OP p. 131)

The rest of *Cuaderno San Martín*'s poems all deal with some aspect of death. A good starting point to analyze this group of poems is "Muertes de Buenos Aires" which is really subdivided into two distinct poems—"La Chacarita" and "La Recoleta." "La Chacarita" refers to Buenos Aires' western cemetery which was opened originally in 1871 due to a severe yellow fever epidemic; it is a resting place for the poor and middle classes. In contrast, "La Recoleta" (located to the north of downtown) is the final resting place of many of the country's most illustrious citizens; it is famous for its wide variety of lavish family pantheons (it is even listed in many guidebooks as a major tourist attraction).

"La Chacarita" is the more extensive of these two works, and is somewhat unique in Borges' poetry due both to the intensity of the harsh apocalyptical vision that it presents (reminiscent of a Bosch painting) and to the sheer accumulation of stark—even shocking—expressionist imagery. The poem begins by explaining how the overwhelmed southern cemetery cried "Enough!" during the yellow fever epidemic, forcing the opening of la Chacarita to hold the overflow of bodies. The disagreeable site was then on the western edge of the city, and noted alternately for dust storms and muddy quagmires depending upon the season. The poet describes a ghostly train heading for the cemetery that is crammed with corpses:

> muertos de barba derrumbada y ojos en vela,
> muertas de carne desalmada y sin magia. (OP p. 120)

These deaths are foul, dirty—dirty like a man's birth: it is a completing of the cycle. The bones plunge into the ground as if they had been flung into an abyss of the sea. Even the cemetery's vegetation has a tortured look, and the surrounding neighborhood—convinced of inevitable doom, symbolized by the cemetery walls—either speeds up its pace of life to arrive at death's door even sooner or tries to blind itself to the reality of death by amusing itself with song or carnaval celebrations. In a parenthesis, the poet quotes from a popular song which serves as a reminder that the very substance of life is death:

> La muerte es vida vivida,
> la vida es muerte que viene. (OP p. 121)

The nearby garbage dump—la Quema—is personified and uses the "death" of objects to mimic the death of people symbolized by the adjoining cemetery. The things that have wound up in the city dump have been contaminated with death from having had contact with humans. The parallel is clear—the cemetery is nothing but a trash heap for humans whose life has been spent. The grave pomp of the funeral processions serves to mask the "shame" of death, for once buried the dead person is reduced to a mere tombstone inscription:

> En tu disciplinado recinto
> la muerte es incolora, hueca, numérica;
> se disminuye a fechas y nombres,
> muertes de la palabra. (OP p. 122)

The poet ends this denunciation of death by directly addressing the cemetery by name, accusing it of being a waste disposal system that is not the door to another life but rather a stagnant dead end. Nonetheless, the poet refuses to surrender to despair maintaining that the cemetery's affirmation of death, in a paradoxical way, really affirms the value of life (symbolized here by the flowering of a single rose).

Death at "La Recoleta" is far less frightful. Old, distinguished families have mass said at the Socorro Church and then participate in a circumspect, dignified burial ceremony. The military burials even have drum rolls to give an added measure of solemnity to the occasion which fits neatly into the family cycle of traditional events—occurring with the same regularity and predictability as a certain sweet dessert that is prepared to celebrate birthdays. The atmosphere at la Recoleta is far more pleasant than at la Chacarita, for here there is a stately gateway to mark the entrance that leads to a park-like world of trees, flowers, and birds. The cemetery turns its back on the northern neighborhood beyond and ignores the wall that Rosas used for executions. The poet does reproach death somewhat in "La Recoleta," speaking of the "nation" of dead that has been dehumanized in death's darkness; but, this is done in more distant historical terms. The main intuition the poet claims to want to communicate is a speculation on why flowers are offered to the dead. The flowers are a fitting accompaniment to the dead because they are silent and will soon shrivel up and die; they are "inoffensive" to the dead person because they do not flaunt the privileges of the living and share the deceased's essential nothingness.

In summary, "La Chacarita" and "La Recoleta" offer two radically different perspectives on death: "La Chacarita" is a tortured vision in which death converts man into cosmic excrement, whereas in "La Recoleta" a calm, more reflective and accepting view of death is presented in which death appears as the natural, necessary, and even desireable conclusion to a forever recurring cycle. Finally, whatever the poet's original intent, one cannot help but see a little bit of social commentary in these twin poems: death (and life) for the poor is brutal, filthy, and animalistic, whereas the rich get a better deal out of the process of dying by turning death into a ritualistic activity whose performance is necessary at periodic intervals to keep the stately family pantheon at la Recoleta adequately stocked.

"La noche que en el sur lo velaron" moves the scene from the cemeteries to the wake that precedes the burial ceremony. The poet uses the occasion to reflect on the unfathomable mystery that death represents: "—misterio cuyo vacante nombre poseo, cuya realidad no abarcamos—" (OP p. 115). On this one occasion a house (that he has never seen before and will never see again) awaits the poet; the atmosphere created here is full of timeless mystery. The poet makes his way very slowly through the streets, streets that echo death's gait because death has eternalized this one night. The poet finally arrives, is gravely received, and in quiet tones he engages those present in intranscendent conversation—the reality of death is too near to speak of more weighty matters. The patio outside appears as an oasis of calm in the "integrity" of the night. During the vigil, the poet is moved by the permanent loss of the eccentricities that had served to distinguish this life from others:

> frecuencias irrecuperables que fueron
> la precisión y la amistad del mundo para él. (OP p. 116)

The poet sees all such life privileges as "miracles"; even the privilege to be at this wake and to be able to speculate on death's unknown qualities is miraculous. Finally fatigue sets in; the physical suffering of those present is aluded to by the reference to Jesus on the cross:

> (El velorio gasta las caras;
> los ojos se nos están muriendo en lo alto como Jesús.) (OP p. 116)

The final section of the poem is devoted to the slow return walk homeward. All of this seems incredible, a dream, not really possible. At least this person's death has given the poet one more memory to store away and the opportunity to more thoroughly savour the southside's quiet streets—the night and its breeze—in these few hours in which death has checked time's flow; under night's protective cloak reality's abundantly ugly face is briefly masked. This poem is praiseworthy for the depth and genuineness of the feelings expressed and for the skillful manner in which the poet makes the reader identify with and participate in this seemingly ordinary experience.

Two of the "death" poems deal directly with Borges' family and close friends. The first of these—"Isidoro Acevedo"—describes the death of his maternal grandfather (in 1905) both from the childhood perspective of the poet himself and also from the perspective of his dying grandfather. In the first segment, the poet confesses that he really did not know his grandfather well as a person—his actual knowledge of him is limited mainly to mere place names and dates. In a conversational tone, the poet procedes to tell the story of the day his grandfather died from the latter's point of view—a perspective that the adults on hand at the time were unaware of. In the next short section of the poem the reader is given necessary historical data—a listing of major events in the dying man's life which will be repeated later in the narrative. The poet remarks that just as some people write verses—like himself—his grandfather conjured up a dream, a dream with which to die. In the fever of his delirium, his grandfather: "congregó los ardientes documentos de su memoria / para fraguar un sueño" (OP p. 113). The effective mention of "documents" serves to give veracity and a sense of palpable reality to the dream that is about to be presented. The grandfather creates a dream of two armies, seeing the faces of his comrades as they were back in his fighting days (not in their present sad reality as faces in rapidly fading daguerreotypes), and briskly reviews the troops before battle. Through the artifice of his dream, the grandfather died gloriously in battle like a true patriot instead of slowly expiring in a quiet, dark room facing a placid garden. Thus,—the poet tells us—the dream served to upgrade the quality of the man's death just as dreams can improve the quality of life for those still living. The poem ends with the poet's own childhood perspective on this death that his innocence refused to let him believe in:

> Yo era chico, yo no sabía entonces de muerte, yo era inmortal;
> (OP p. 114)

The poet's purpose in recounting this novel version of the historical reality of his grandfather's death is to preserve the dying man's ephemeral dream permanently in the world of poetry: what is stored in memory and is even occasionally remembered is not totally dead. This is the tenuous form of immortality to which the poet himself aspires.

"A Francisco López Merino" was also born out of a concrete experience in Borges' personal life—the suicide of this valued friend at age twenty-four (May 20, 1928). While wishing that something could have been done to prevent the tragedy, the poet poses the question as to whether life is really worth living. His conclusion is that life is justified in music, trees, fountains, love: "los cargados minutos / por los que se salva el honor de la realidad" (OP p. 126). The poet consoles himself with the thought that his friend took his own life in order to be able to forge his own personal image of death (rather than let death just happen of its own accord). In this personal vision of death, the young poet sought a friendly forgetting of the world, where forgetting would be like a blessing. In the phrase "nos queda un sedimento de eternidad," the poet expresses the desire that something should remain of each person's life as a "sediment" of eternity: "como los versos en que siempre estás esperándonos" (OP p. 126). Again, poetry is suggested as one possible form of this so sought after fragment of immortality that the poet ardently longs for.

The poem "A la doctrina de pasión de tu voz" (suppressed by Borges in the 1967 edition of *Obra poética*) continues expounding on the theme that life is somehow worthwhile despite its many negative aspects. The text itself is left open to several interpretations by the reader. In a more literal reading, the "voice" that is so praised in the poem can be a real voice symbolizing the liberating power of music or of love. On another plane, the voice can be seen to symbolize the pure feelings expressed in poetry; this poetic voice represents both love and true happiness—by the sheer virtue of its existence, life takes on meaning and is worthwhile. It is a poem that strongly affirms life in a book heavily weighted down with the theme of death. The poem is laden with Christian imagery (the accumulative effect of words such as "doctrina," "pasión," "creer," and "vocación," is difficult to ignore); this would seem to leave the poem open to a religious interpretation. However, Borges has no truly "religious" poems in the strictest sense of the word, because for Borges religion implies the acceptance of dogma; the cornerstone of Borges' personal philosophy of life is the total rejection of all forms of dogmatic thought. Here the poet is using the dense Christian imagery more as a rhetorical device that seems appropriate to the content rather than trying to express any religious feelings.

The texts of *Cuaderno San Martín* reveal a warm, sensitive poet that expresses in a low-key, conversational style genuine fears and hopes concerning death which is presented as the most fundamental mystery in all men's lives. The poet sees all life as a precious gift, a privilege to be grateful for and to be lived to its fullest potential. Death may be inevitable, but can be combated with memory; thus, in the "nostalgia" poems memory can eternalize the past by making it a timeless present. Dreams and fantasies are other powerful weapons that can create a mythical, atemporal world, by stopping time's flow and preventing death from casting the past into the total oblivion of the forgotten.

Notes

[1] Jorge Luis Borges, "An Autobiographical Essay," *The Aleph and Other Stories 1933–1969*, Norman Thomas di Giovanni, editor and translator (New York: E.P. Dutton, 1978), p. 232–233.

[2] Jorge Luis Borges, *Obra poética 1923–1964* (Buenos Aires: Emecé Editores, S.A., 1964), p. 103. Hereafter cited in text as OP.

6
The Myth of the "Lyrical Hiatus": 1930–1960

Although Borges published no new separate books of poetry between the 1929 publication of *Cuaderno San Martín* and the appearance of *El hacedor* in 1960, this was still an active period in his poetic production. Critics—such as Zunilda Gertel—have referred to this period as Borges' "lyrical hiatus." In the "Nota preliminar" to her book *Borges y su retorno a la poesía*, Gertel describes the 1930–1960 period in Borges' career as a poet as follows: "Un quiebre en su producción poética durante el lapso de un cuarto de siglo y el escéptico prólogo de *Poemas* llevó a generalizar la afirmación de que Borges había agotado su lírica."[1] The "skeptical prologue" to *Poemas* (1943) cannot be seen as a proof that Borges' poetic inspiration had run dry since this prologue is just a reiteration of Borges' concept of the art of poetry that was expressed in the 1923 prologue to *Fervor de Buenos Aires* and in the Edward FitzGerald quote that Borges used to set the tone for *Cuaderno San Martín*. Although Gertel is cognizant of the fact that Borges published many poems during the 1930–1960 period, and that he made numerous revisions to his previous work, she keeps using terms such as "quiebre" (break, gap) and "hiato" (hiatus) to refer to the 1930–1960 segment in Borges' poetic production. Gertel mitigates the harshness of this by stating: "Nos proponemos demonstrar la unidad en la trayectoria de la poesía borgiana e interpretar este hiato como una auténtica concentración en la actividad creadora" (ZG p. 9).

It is evident that Gertel views the 1930–1960 period as one of theoretical retrenchment, a sort of bridge between what she judges as his less successful ultraist years and the higher quality of his more poetically prolific years beginning with the publication of *El hacedor* in 1960.

Gertel believes that this increase in quality is due to Borges' perfection and use of a "personal" or "private" symbol: "Creemos poder demostrar la razón del retorno a la lírica en el hallazgo del símbolo personal o 'privado,' elemento conductor de la inquietud metafísica que el poeta no logró expresar en su época ultraista" (ZG p. 9). Near the end of her study, Gertel restates this conclusion: "El retorno de Borges a la lírica se realiza cuando el poeta halla en el mundo mítico de su poesía el símbolo conductor de la inquietud metafísica" (ZG p. 134). This "private symbol" is based on the harmonious reconciliation of "clashing opposites" that restores a basic order and unity to Borges' fragmentary and chaotic vision of the universe. This is undoubtedly one of the most important conceits that is constantly recurring in Borges' poetry, and an adequate comprehension of it facilitates gaining a full understanding of Borges' poetry. Nonetheless, it is clearly present in Borges' earlier poetry ("Forjadura" in *Fervor de Buenos Aires* and the "La Chacarita" section of "Muertes de Buenos Aires" from *Cuaderno San Martín* are good examples of this important conceit at work in Borges' earlier work). Therefore, the presence of the "private symbol" in *El hacedor* cannot totally explain the increase in Borges' poetic production starting in the late 1950's, nor does it explain his proportionately decreased production of new poems during the 1930–1958 period. In short, Gertel's emphasis on finding this "private symbol" as the key to *El hacedor* lead her to downgrade the importance of the 1930–1960 period in Borges' career.

If Gertel's perception of this period is somewhat questionable, that of most other critics is far worse; a couple of brief quotes from Rodríguez Monegal will suffice to sum up this general lack of comprehension. Speaking of this period in Borges' career, Rodríguez Monegal states: "Borges himself was a bit unsure about what to do next. He had come to realize that poetry would never be his chief concern or his lasting claim to fame."[2] Rodríguez Monegal provides no proof as to how he knows that Borges came to these conclusions. Speaking of the 1930's period in Borges' career, Rodríguez Monegal states somewhat dogmatically: "He had come to believe that he would never be a really good poet and had practically ceased to write verses. Perhaps he sincerely believed his poetry was of no consequence" (RM p. 358). However, Borges' humility in evaluating his own work is legend; it begins in print with the "A quien leyere" note that helps to preface *Fervor de Buenos Aires* and is a constant in his career with respect to both his poetry and his prose. Therefore, Borges' own reticence to see value in and praise his own work cannot be seen as proof that the writer actually believed that he was incapable of writing any more quality poetry. If anything, during the 1930's Borges shows very clear hesitation to cultivate the literary form for which he is now most famous—the short story. Thus, a reappraisal of the 1930–1960 period in Borges' work is necessary to a full understanding of the unfolding of his career as a poet.

The years between the 1929 publication of *Cuaderno San Martín* and the 1943 publication of *Poemas* were among the most important in Borges' literary career. He began the decade of the 1930's with the publication of the work that he had for so long thought about writing—*Evaristo Carriego* (1930); the money from the prize he won for *Cuaderno San Martín* helped provide a financial cushion for the writing of this much less successful work. Undaunted by the lack of success of *Evaristo Carriego* among critics, the buying public, and even his inner group of friends, Borges continued to write essays, publishing the first edition of *Discusión* in 1932. For many years Borges had been toying with the idea of expressing in prose—in the form of short stories—many of the same preoccupations that are expressed in his poetry. In his "Autobiographical Essay" Borges tells us that for years he had thought that the short story was beyond his powers: "It took me some six years, from 1927–1933, to go from that all too self-conscious sketch

'Hombres pelearon' to my first outright short story, 'Hombre de la esquina rosada' (Streetcorner Man)."[3] He goes on to state that due partly to shyness and partly to the feeling that "the story was a bit beneath me," he signed the work with a pen name—Francisco Bustos; it appeared in the tabloid daily *Crítica* in 1933. The years 1933–1934 saw Borges publish many more brief narratives in *Crítica*'s *Revista Multicolor de los Sábados*; although that was not his original plan, Borges made a collection of these pieces and published them in 1935 under the title of *Historia universal de la infamia*. His next story, "The Approach to al-Mu'tasim" was written in 1935 and slipped inconspicuously (disguised as a book review) into his next collection of essays, *Historia de la eternidad*, published in 1936. Clearly, what Borges was trying to do with these pieces was to develop a new mode of expression and then to experiment with its possibilities. The necessity of finding such new avenues of expression became evident to Borges by the mid 1920's; in poems such as "Mi vida entera" in *Luna de enfrente*, the poet already feels that he has done it all—thus, in poems such as this, one can find hints of Borges' incipient short-story career. In an interview with Rita Guibert published in 1968, Borges reminds his audience of his belief that writers have only a few essential themes about which to write: "Si usted lee esa compilación que se titula *Obra poética*, verá que yo tengo muy pocos temas."[4]

By the time Borges published *Cuaderno San Martín* in 1929, he was convinced that he had already addressed those essential themes in some fashion. His decision at this point was to revise carefully and improve his previous collections of poetry rather than to write a large number of new poems. The new poems Borges did write in this period are more dense, distilled products that try to explore different perspectives of those same themes. In the Guibert interview Borges provides further clarification:

> Es como si me hubiera pasado la vida entera escribiendo siete u ocho poemas y ensayando diversas variaciones, como si cada libro fuera un borrador del libro anterior. Pero esto no me avergüenza; es prueba de que escribo con sinceridad, puesto que no sería difícil buscar otros

> temas. Si vuelvo a esos temas es porque siento que son esenciales y también porque siento que no he cumplido con ellos . . . , tengo como una deuda. (RG p. 339)

This "debt" that Borges feels he owes to his small corpus of essential themes leads him not only to rewrite old poems and produce lesser and greater variations of these themes in new poems, but also spurs him on to labor with expressing these same themes in his essays and finally in the writing of his short stories. In this context the temporary switch of the bulk of Borges' literary production from poetry to the short story is easily explained by the writer's desire to use all of the literary genres at his command as a means to reach the principal goal of his writing—the most effective expression possible of a limited number of basic themes. After using poetry as his principal means of expression during the 1920's, Borges decided to experiment with the short story's possibilities in the 1930's and 1940's. By the time Borges published *El Aleph* in 1949, he had already thoroughly explored the short story as a vehicle for elaborating and seeking fresh perspectives on his basic themes, and was ready to make poetry his first priority again—poetry would dominate Borges new literary production during the 1950's, 1960's, 1970's, and into the 1980's. Again, it must be repeated that virtually all of Borges' recurrent themes were already present in *Fervor de Buenos Aires*; the writer has spent his life expanding on them in poetry, essays, and short stories. In the same interview with Rita Guibert, Borges emphasizes the embryonic nature of *Fervor de Buenos Aires*:

> Pero creo que yo estoy en ese libro, y que todo lo que he hecho después está entre líneas en él. Me reconozco más que en otros libros, aunque no creo que el lector pueda reconocerme. Pienso que ahí he estado a punto de escribir lo que escribiría treinta o cuarenta años después. (RG p. 338)

After the 1929 publication of *Cuaderno San Martín*, Borges' next poems were written in 1934. Originally entitled "Prose poems for I.J.," they were later simply retitled as "Two English

Poems" (the initials were later changed to "S.D." and then again changed to the full name of yet another woman—it is best to see these works as "generic" love poems). Borges wrote the poems in English not because he did not feel capable of writing any more poems in Spanish, but rather to preserve a measure of his personal privacy. These self-revealing poems expose raw feelings of loneliness and longings for romantic love that the poet wanted to express in writing but felt too timid to do so in his native language—thereby baring his soul to his Argentine contemporaries. By choosing English as a mode of expression, the poems were relegated to the realm of personal eccentricity, and remained relatively "private" until the development of a large English-speaking reading audience (which did not occur until the 1960's).

The first of these love poems in English expresses the poet's desire to be loved, to be romantically desired; it begins:

> The useless dawn finds me in a deserted street- corner; I have outlived the night[5]

The setting is reminiscent of many of Borges' previous poems—dawn catches the poet on a particular Buenos Aires street corner. Here the dawn is "useless" because it only serves to destroy his night fantasy world by imposing the light of reality; the night is a repository of positive things: "laden with things unlikely and desirable." For the poet the night is full of "mysterious gifts" that are "half given away, half withheld." The things that might ordinarily provide him with contentment—friends, music, tobacco—now disgust him and only serve to remind him of his basic lack of fulfillment caused by the absence of a person to love. The poet is left with haunting memories of his last affair:

> I turn them over in the dawn, I lose them, I find them; I tell them to the few stray dogs and to the few stray stars of the dawn.
> (OP p. 141)

The poet concludes that mere memories are insufficient; he

desperately needs the real thing, not these "illustrious toys." The poet's search for a concrete person to love and to be loved by becomes even more desperate in the second English poem. After asking the rhetorical question "What can I hold you with," the poet frankly lists the positive and the negative things that he has to offer. On the negative side are loneliness, ghostly memories of the past, bitterness, and "the loyalty of a man who has never been loyal." The adjectives that the poet applies to the city streets—"lean," "desperate," "jagged"—really describe his own being. On the positive side, the poet offers his mystery woman the insight of his books, a modicum of humor and manliness, beautiful visions of the past symbolized by the yellow rose, and new perspectives on herself in the form of self revelations. Most of all the poet is willing to offer the very essence of his being:

> I offer you that kernel of myself that I have saved,
>   somehow—the central heart that deals not in words, traffics not
> with dreams and is untouched by time, by joy, by adversities.
> (OP p. 142)

When the poet confesses: "I am trying to bribe you" (OP p. 143); the extreme depth of his despair becomes evident.

Borges' next poem—"Insomnio"—first appeared in print in *Sur*'s December 1936 issue; the poem actually corresponds to a period in the poet's life when he was suffering from a very bad case of insomnia. It clearly foreshadows the story "Funes, el Memorioso" (which first appeared in *La nación* in 1942); both the poem and the subsequently written story elaborate on the theme of endless, uncontrollable lucidity. The poet begins "Insomnia" with the reflection that the night must really be sturdy to enable to survive the terrible things in the world that flood his consciousness. In the second stanza the poet projects his own tiredness upon the things that have tired him out (this section can be read as an actual linear recounting of Borges' train trip from the summer heat of Buenos Aires to his vacation retreat in Adrogué). Despite his physical exhaustion, the poet cannot sleep:

> El universo de esta noche tiene la vastedad
> del olvido y la precisión de la fiebre. (OP p. 137)

As the poet vainly tries to fall asleep, he is tortured by multitudinous visions of reality that refuse to leave his consciousness; they are represented first by a mirror that duplicates—and threatens—his physical body, then by the house's patio which also seems to multiply along with an endless procession of city neighborhoods. Relentlessly, consciousness persists:

> En vano espero
> las desintegraciones y los símbolos que preceden
> al sueño. (OP p. 138)

The fragmentary, fantastic world of dreams is again seen as being far superior to objective reality. Even realities that the poet usually enjoys such as a bird's song or moonlight reflected in a pond are now sources of displeasure:

> (He odiado el agua crapulosa de un charco,
> he aborrecido en el atardecer el canto del pájaro.) (OP p.138)

Meanwhile, the poet is all too aware of the constant flow of time; he feels it in the circulation of his blood, a metaphor which he immediately extends to the cosmic level of the rotation of the planets. Time's destructive nature is again emphasized by the measurement of its flow by the constant progression of dental caries—an ugly reality symbolic of decay and death. The poet now curses his beloved streets in Buenos Aires' southern neighborhoods and the vast expanses of the pampas; both now refuse to leave his memory, and he is a lone sentinel as the world slumbers. The poet is struck by the thought of a horrible form of immortality in which one would be condemned to be a perpetual witness to all that is in the universe, unable ever to banish it from one's consciousness. Dawn—whose ordinarily benign clouds are now perceived as being hateful—finally arrives to find the poet with his eyelids tightly shut, but still unable to fall asleep and to replace an all too present reality with blissful dreams.

Borges' next poem—"La noche cíclica"—which dates from 1940, is a concrete example of his theoretical belief that a poem's structure should correspond to and complement its meaning. This poem, whose theme is cyclical time, has a repetitive cyclical structure of rhymed (abba) fourteen syllable quatrains; the added touch of making the first line identical to the last implies that the poem will continue on infinitely, reinforcing the poem's thematic stress on time's cyclical nature. The first quatrain is a straightfoward statement of the basic theme: "Los astros y los hombres vuelven cíclicamente" (OP p. 144). The mention of Pythagoras and then Rome serves to underscore the age and remoteness of this time-wearied concept, and to pave the way for the mention of the centaur and the minotaur, which in turn serve to deny linear time by conjuring up the world of myth to the readers' consciousness. The third quatrain's first line ("Volverá toda noche de insomnio: minuciosa.") is a reminder of the poet's preoccupation with insomnia and more importantly a statement of how history is constantly repeating itself with maddening sameness. (In later printings, David Hume replaces Nietzsche in the last line of the third quatrain as the provider of some of the poem's philosophical base—the reason is chiefly political. Borges originally greatly admired Nietzsche's works but later wished to put some distance between himself and a man whom he later associated with fascism.) The poet's nocturnal city wanderings also provide proof for the theory of cyclical time: no matter where he walks, he basically winds up in the same spot—with its fig tree, colored wall, and broken sidewalk. But, while the cycle provides others with money or love, the poet has to content himself with Buenos Aires' streets and lingering memories of the past; this is a clear reference to the poet's inability to find a satisfying love relationship—the theme of the "Two English Poems" as well as being a constant obsession from the poems of *Fervor de Buenos Aires* onward. The poem's final quatrain takes the reader from the present moment of the poet's Buenos Aires wanderings back to remote time symbolized by Anaxagoras. The point made is that poetry is also cyclical; poets repeat the same themes with minor variations, but always return to certain constants with mathematical precision. By extension, this poem represents Borges' own poetic output which is basically cyclical in nature due to his repeated re-elaborations of a limited number of themes.

Martin Stabb criticizes "La noche cíclica" somewhat harshly, calling it "cold," "overly intellectual," and "bookish."[6] On the other hand, Zunilda Gertel praises it—she calls it Borges' first "metaphysical poem." She goes on to state that Borges: "No encuentra aún el símbolo conductor, pero ya el pensamiento metafísico fluye como auténtica poesía y no como mera exposición filosófica" (ZG p. 126). Borges effectively expressed metaphysical preoccupations in all three of his poetry collections of the 1920's; whether "La noche cíclica" is more "authentic" poetry or more "metaphysical" than what Borges had written previously is open to debate. In addition, Gertel sees "newness" in Borges' use of a more traditional structure for this poem:

> Es preciso destacar—si tenemos presente el absoluto rechazo anterior de Borges con respecto a la métrica regular y a la rima—que el poeta escribe su primera poesía metafísica en cuartetos alejandrinos con rima consonante . . . (ZG p. 127)

However, there is little novelty at all here. Borges opened the door to the validity of the use of traditional forms as early as his 1923 prologue to *Fervor de Buenos Aires,* and actually wrote poems using such forms in both *Luna de enfrente* and *Cuaderno San Martín* among which are some of the poet's most famous works ("El general Quiroga va en coche al muere" and "La fundación mítica de Buenos Aires" are two good examples—and there are more). Gertel summarizes her analysis of "La noche cíclica" by stating: "No hallamos aún los símbolos del laberinto y la identidad en el poema, pero es notorio el fluir de la inquietud metafísica" (ZG p. 128). However, both the labyrinth and identity (both personal identity and one's own identity compared to "the other") appear as frequent motifs in *Fervor de Buenos Aires*. The most obvious manifestation of the labyrinth motif in Borges' first published book of poems are the streets of Buenos Aires themselves. Moreover, the poem "La noche cíclica" itself devotes an entire quatrain to highlight the similarity of the city streets to a labyrinth:

> Las plazas agravadas por la noche sin dueño
> Son los patios profundos de un árido palacio
> Y las calles unánimes que engendran el espacio
> Son corredores de vago miedo y de sueño. (OP p. 145)

The "arid palace" with its endless "corridors" on the simplest level can symbolize the poet's house, but on another plain they are clearly a metaphor for the labyrinth—this quatrain foreshadows the atmosphere that Borges would later create in "La casa de Asterión" (first published in *Los anales de Buenos Aires* in 1947), a short story in which the labyrinth motif is the very substance of the entire work. In summary, it can be said that "La noche cíclica" is indeed a good poem, in part because its structure is well suited to its content; it is a well-balanced content whose stress is on cyclical time and the repetitive nature of human existence. In addition, the poem, far from being cold, gives the reader a glimpse of Borges' personal sense of loneliness by relating the more abstract metaphysical concepts to something more personal and concrete that the reader can identify with. The chaos implied by the labyrinth motif is balanced by the order imposed by cyclical time and exemplified by the repetitive rhythms of the poems itself.

These were traumatic years in Borges' personal life, but the writer kept the most direct references to his own private hell out of his literature. An exception to this is a 1940 prose piece with an attached poem fragment (not allowed published until 1973) in which the poet describes his own "suicide" at the Adrogué Hotel (RM p. 348–349). To Borges' chronic depression about his inability to establish a meaningful love relationship were added a series of traumas that shook the foundations of his existence. His paternal grandmother—Fanny Haslam—

died slowly and painfully in 1935; Borges greatly respected her, and she had formed part of the family household for decades. The household suffered more turmoil when Borges' father died in 1938; although in a sense liberated from his father's shadow, Borges now was head of the household and had to face the family's worsening financial plight. Since 1937 he had been forced to accept a dreary position—the first full-time job in his entire life—at a small municipal branch library where he greatly disliked the majority of his co-workers and felt utterly wasted and frustrated. In his "Autobiographical Essay" the poet sums it up: "I stuck out the library for about nine years. They were nine years of solid unhappiness" (AE p. 241). Also, late in 1938 after his father's death, Borges suffered a head wound in an "accident" (a suicide attempt?) that gave him blood poisoning; he briefly hovered near death with a high fever and delirium. For a short time he feared that he might have lost his creative powers. In addition, the poet was depressed about the success of Nazism in Europe during those same years; he wrote many articles denouncing the fascist tide. However, the immediate catalyst for this rash of suicidal thoughts was probably Lugones' 1938 suicide; at the time of Lugones' death, Borges wrote laudatory articles on the poet he had once vilified.

It is in this context that the 1942 poem "Del infierno y del cielo" should be seen. The poem is the poet's personal vision of immortality in which the traditional views of what heaven and hell may be like are all summarily rejected one after the other. Instead the poet offers the vision he was able to glimpse in a dream; heaven and hell consist of nothing more than the eternal contemplation of a never-changing face producing never-ending ecstasy for the just and the perpetual torture of unwanted consciousness for the condemned. This vision of heaven and hell is attractive to the poet because it implies the total destruction of time; those who contemplate the eternal face will inhabit a changeless world of perpetual present time, a mythical dream world. Also present in this poem is the theme of "the other"; the face to be contemplated after death could be that of one's lover, one's own face, or a likeness of oneself.

Borges presents a variant of this same theme of reducing the universe to a likeness or double of oneself in the epilogue found at the conclusion of *El hacedor*.

One of the finest poems that Borges composed during this period was "Poema conjetural," which was written in 1943. Its immediate inspiration was probably more related to fascism's triumphs during World War II than to his ancestor Francisco Narciso de Laprida, who was killed fighting for freedom over a century before the writing of the poem and is nominally the poem's chief protagonist. This preoccupation with the current political events is evident in terse lines such as: "Vencen los bárbaros, los gauchos vencen" (OP p. 148). However, the poem's principal purpose is to give a concrete example of how the concept of cyclical history actually works in the life of an individual; Laprida himself becomes symbolic of any man and all men whose fate it is to die for their ideals. The poet chooses the most dramatic moment in this repeating cycle—the hero's death—to furnish the poem's raw material. The poem begins with Laprida's defeat during his last battle; the poet gallops off alone to face his destiny. The first person narration provides great dramatic impact with its immediateness. The poet includes lines such as "Yo, que estudié las leyes y los cánones" (OP p. 148), to emphasize that Laprida is the symbol of reason, law, order, justice, and idealism while the barbarians—the gauchos—represent the forces of evil, chaos, and destruction. The captain mentioned is a character lifted out of Dante's *Purgatory* and was killed in battle in 1289. Thus, Laprida is merely reliving the destiny that others have already faced in earlier circles of history just as other men face similar destinies in the twentieth century. It is the poet's way of showing that the present consists of reliving the past; all variations are minor. One hero is all heroes; one man is all men. For this reason Borges even translated a line into Spanish that is lifted right out of Dante's *Purgatory* (V,99): "huyendo a pie y ensangrentando el llano" (OP p. 148). By repeating itself, the poetry corresponds to the protagonists' recurring destiny. The reason Borges chose to quote from Dante rather than some other author is a good example of how he delights in taking material recently read and enjoyed, and finding a way to work it into his own writing in some fashion. In his "Autobiographical Essay," Borges tells us how (near the time this poem was written) he made the boring trips to his municipal library job more bearable by reading Dante's *Divine Comedy* (AE p. 242). Borges' protagonist—Laprida—is aware that he will share the same fate as Dante's character; he freely accepts this destiny as the natural conclusion to his own life cycle—the key to the reason for his own existence. In the midst of this philosophizing, the poet succeeds in maintaining and building up the suspense and mystery with lines such as: "Oigo los cascos de mi caliente muerte que me busca" (OP p. 148). With remarkable conciseness, the apocalyptical horsemen bearing death are reduced to the sound of hoof beats. As Laprida savours the joy of comprehending his own destiny within the overall scheme of the universe, he speculates that he would have preferred to have lead the peaceful life of a man of learning and books:

> Yo que anhelé ser otro, ser un hombre
> de sentencias, de libros, de dictámenes, (OP p. 149)

This obvious role reversal is Borges' way of expressing his own personal desire to have been a man of action like Laprida rather than the learned man of letters. Nonetheless, Laprida's resigned but simultaneously exuberant acceptance of his destiny mirrors the poet's own process of finally coming to terms with and accepting both his slot in historical time and the role that fate has alotted to him. The labyrinth theme is also clearly present in "Poema conjetural"; life is a disorderly puzzle—finding the key to the riddle is man's chief life task. The poet defines life as "el laberinto múltiple de pasos" whose goal is to discover "la recóndita clave de mis años" (OP p. 149). The reference to "mi insospechado rostro eterno" clearly ties this poem to Borges' view of immortality in "Del infierno y del cielo"; the protagonist Laprida is drawing the last lines that will forever shape his eternity. Finally, the last six verses are a well-realized dramatic tour de force: the attackers get closer and closer but the narrator continues to tell his story as the shadows of the lances close in on him. He tells of the first blow that he feels, the steel that penetrates his chest, and finally the sensation of the "intimate" knife at his throat. The poem has ended, there is blank silence on the page, the narrator is dead.[7]

Shortly after publishing "Poema conjetural" in *La nación* (July 4, 1943), Borges published the volume entitled *Poemas* (1922–1943) which included his three previous books of poetry in addition to the poems that he had written more recently. Thus, in this first lap of Borges' slowed poetic production, he wrote eight new poems; he inserted two of these inconspicuously in *Luna de enfrente* and grouped the other six under the heading "Otros poemas." (Borges' ninth new poem during this period was the 1940 surpressed fragment dealing with suicide.) However, the new poems represent only a small fraction of Borges' poetic activity during the 1930–1943 period, for during these years, the poet directed his poetic talents at pruning, revising, and generally upgrading the quality of his previous work. The scope of these revisions is noteworthy. First he deleted seventeen poems (eight from *Fervor de Buenos Aires*, eight from *Luna de enfrente,* and one from *Cuaderno San Martín*). Nineteen poems were slightly revised, twenty-one others received moderate revisions, and twenty-six poems were revised extensively. (Norman Thomas Di Giovanni's classification system is again used here: minor revisions affect one tenth or fewer lines, moderate revisions affect more than one tenth but less than one third of the lines, and extensive revisions affect one third or more lines.)[8]

In summary, during the years 1930–1943 Borges revised a total of sixty-six of his previously written poems (forty-seven of which received either moderate or extensive revisions) in addition to composing at least eight new poems. To call these active years of poetic preoccupation a "lyrical hiatus" is not accurate. The fact that Borges did not publish his new poetry as a separate book, compounded with the general tendency of ignoring the importance of the very large corpus of revised texts, has led to the myth that Borges had simply run dry as a poet. The simultaneous appearance and success of the poet's short stories also served effectively to mask the extent of his poetic endeavors. A constant desire to rewrite and improve upon his previously written poetry and prose is a hallmark of Borges' literary career.

The period between the 1929 publication of *Cuaderno San Martín* and the 1943 appearance of *Poemas* was almost incredibly prolific. Borges produced three books of essays—*Evaristo Carriego* (1930), *Discusión* (1932), *Historia de la eternidad* (1936)—, published two short story collections—*Historia universal de la infamia* (1935), *El jardín de senderos que se bifurcan* (1941)—, and worked in collaboration with others to publish works such as the *Classical Anthology of Argentine Literature* (1937, with Pedro Henríquez Ureña), *Antología de la literatura fantástica* (1940, with Adolfo Bioy Casares and Silvina Ocampo), and *Seis problemas para don Isidro Parodi* (1942, with Adolfo Bioy Casares). In addition, Borges churned out numerous articles for the literary supplement to the Buenos Aires newspaper *Crítica*, wrote the bi-weekly foreign books and authors page for the magazine *El hogar* (1936–1939), and wrote many pieces for Victoria Ocampo's prestigious literary magazine *Sur*. In 1936 he founded a new literary magazine—*Destiempo*—with Adolfo Bioy Casares (it lasted only three issues). On top of this Borges did translations into Spanish of works by such diverse authors such as Faulkner, Virginia Woolf, Melville, Gide, and Kafka. Considering the personal turmoil Borges suffered during these years (in addition to the political turmoil of the times), his literary output was extraordinary. It is easy to see how the author's relatively modest poetry output was virtually lost in this deluge of published work.

Borges republished his poetry again in 1954—*Poemas 1923–1953*. This collection contains only four new poems compared with the work's 1943 edition. The poet continued to refine his previous texts: he deleted one more poem from *Fervor de Buenos Aires*, gave minor revisions to twenty-one poems, moderately revised two other poems, and gave extensive revisions to two others—a total of twenty-five revised poems and four new ones. Borges also wrote some other poems during this period that were not included in the "Otras composiciones" section of *Poemas 1923–1953*. *La nación* refused to print "El puñal" for political reasons; the poem could be construed to condone the assasination of tyrants—such as Perón (it is equally a reminder of Borges' fascination with the tools of violence and the men of action that those tools imply; "El puñal" also repeats the theme of the part symbolizing the whole—the dagger in the poet's drawer is simultaneously all the daggers that ever existed in the universe). This poem was finally published in *Marcha* (June 25, 1954) in Uruguay; it also appears in the 1969 Emecé printing of *El otro el mismo*. In addition, Borges published several poems under fanciful pseudonyms in the pages of *Los anales de Buenos Aires* during the late 1940's; he finally republished some of these in *El hacedor* in 1960.

Perón's ascent to power in 1946 resulted in Borges being dismissed from his municipal library job; the poet declined the offer of a substitute position as poultry and rabbit inspector at the local markets. Actually, it was a blessing in disguise because it forced Borges to overcome his fear of public speaking. He accepted an English literature teaching position at the Asociación Argentina de Cultura Inglesa and agreed to do a lecture series on the literature of the United States at the Colegio Libre de Estudios Superiores. This marked the beginning of Borges' active career as a lecturer—a career which would continue unbroken for decades. In addition to continuing his journalistic career, during the 1943–1954 period Borges also wrote two fine collections of short stories—*Ficciones* (1944) and two editions of *El Aleph* (1949 and 1952)—, published a collection of essays—*Otras inquisiciones* (1952)—, and produced a variety of works with the collaboration of others. At this point, one might note with some irony the presence of a two-decade "narrative hiatus" in Borges' career, since he did not publish any new collections of short stories between the 1949 publication of *El Aleph* and the appearance of *El informe de*

Brodie in 1970 (Borges republished the revised and expanded versions of *El Aleph* and *Ficciones* in 1952 and 1956 respectively). The 1950's would see Borges writing more and more poetry and less prose—a process that would accelerate in the 1960's and 1970's.

A brief examination of the four new poems published in *Poemas 1923–1953* is in order. The first of these—"Poema del cuarto elemento" first appeared in 1944. The poem—written in rhymed quatrains (abba)—is an ode to water and its many varied forms or "metaphors"—clouds, rain, oceans, rivers, tears. The many references to mythological characters and philosophers give water magical qualities—it is a mythical substance that exists in an eternal present (the same water that washed Christ's body also washed the poet's father's body). Water participates in cyclical time (it is different and the same) and its smallest quantity implies the whole; therefore all men have bathed in the Ganges. The poem is resplendent with some of Borges' preferred motifs: the labyrinth (here the sea is an "open labyrinth"), dreams, nightmares, and shining knives. The last quatrain is a direct prayer from the poet—who mentions his own name—to water, which entreats the water to remember to annoit his lips at the hour of his death. This surprise ending, in which the third person verbs forms and the second person singular "tú" form—used to address the sea—are suddenly replaced by the first person "yo," reveals the poet's continuing preoccupation with his own death. The hymn of praise to water turns into a pretext to express the poet's personal anguish.

The poet's obsession with his own death appears in a different guise in the poem "A un poeta menor de la antología." In it the poet worries about his place in history and the possibility of total oblivion. Superficially, the poem is supposed to be dealing with the Greek poet Theocritus (it is not by sheer chance that Borges chose this poet—Theocritus is known for mixing reality and fantasy in his pastoral poems). Borges asks the Greek poet about the fate of the daily occurrences that made up Theocritus' life; the living poet provides the answer for his deceased comrade:

> El río numerable de los años
> los ha perdido; eres una palabra en un índice. (OP p. 152)

While others got glory and monuments, all that remains of Theocritus are a few anthologized poems. However, Borges admonishes him not to fault the gods for their stinginess, for those who are given glory have their reputations ultimately tarnished under the bright light of passing time's scrutiny. Therefore, Theocritus will remain a sweet voice in beautiful twilight—faint but eternally remembered. This fate—to have the details of his biography forgotten and to be saved from total oblivion by a few of his best poems—is clearly the one that Borges desires; the poet restates this hope in the closing lines of his prologue to *Obra poética 1923–1964*.

"Página para recordar al Coronel Suárez, vencedor en Junín" makes use of one of Borges' most common literary devices—the poet uses raw material from his own family's life experiences and projects it onto a universal plane. The poet believes that the many small miseries that made up his great-grandfather's life are irrelevant—what is important is that he had one glorious moment fighting for freedom at the battle of Junín which justified his entire existence:

> Qué importan las penurias, el desierto,
> la humillación de envejecer, . . .
>
> * * *
>
> Qué importa el tiempo sucesivo si en él
> hubo una plenitud, un éxtasis, una tarde. (OP p. 154)

The destructive flow of time does not matter if in it there is something of lasting value: the bloody battle in which Coronel Suárez was a hero is his eternal "rose." The poet takes obvious pleasure in describing the battle, going through the day's events just as if they were now parading through his grandfather's consciousness. The poet envisions the "furious labyrinth" of the fighting armies, the joy of victory, the post-battle fatigue that sets in, the dying soldiers left in the swamps, Bolívar making historic pronouncements, and the simple pleasures of water and wine (which represent a return from the mythical plane to small daily realities). The poet has his great-grandfather directly address the reader in the poem's final summation: one battle for freedom is all battles for freedom, one hero is all heroes. The battle is eternal:

> Junín son dos civiles que en una esquina maldicen a un tirano,
> o un hombre oscuro que se muere en la cárcel. (OP p. 156)

The poet's ancestor is the archetype of the freedom fighter whose struggle is endless; thus, the poet moves from the small detail (Junín) to a universal level. The date of the poem (1953) makes it a clear statement against Perón in particular, but this does not detract from its more generalized denunciation of all forms of totalitarianism.

In "Mateo XXV,30" the poet is struck with a vision of his own presence at the Last Judgment brought on by the noise, smoke, and whistles of the trains at Constitution Station in Buenos Aires. In this vision, a voice from the center of the poet's being speaks out and gives a long chaotic ennumeration of all the elements that have made up his life, and lists all of the gifts that have been bestowed upon him (this poem can be seen as an intensification of the poem "Mi vida entera" from *Luna de enfrente*). The reference to "álgebra y fuego" can symbolize reason and passion on one level, but they are also a metaphor for the essence of what good poetry should be—calculated physical construction and sound thought (algebra) meshed effectively with pure emotion (fire). The reference to being forced to eat the food that heroes are made of—defeat and humiliation—is an allusion to his feeling of personal oppression under the Perón regime. Finally, the voice concludes that despite the bountiful gifts given to the poet, he has still been unable to write *the* poem:

> Has gastado los años y te han gastado,
> Y todavía no has escrito el poema. (OP p. 158)

This again serves to explain why Borges chose to spend so many years revising his previous poetry rather than churning out reams of new poetry. By 1929 he had already written about all his essential themes, but he was not satisfied with the overall quality of his work. His moral duty as a poet would be to strive for absolutes—the perfect poem that would embody all of his essential themes in glorious harmony—knowing full well that the writing of a perfect poem is not possible. Nonetheless, like Sisyphus, Borges doggedly applies himself to this impossible task. Like his ancestor Laprida, Borges has discovered the secret key to the meaning of his existence in striving for unattainable poetic absolutes. Borges knows he will never write *the* poem, but that knowledge does not detract from either the dignity or the necessity of the endeavor. This poem instead of symbolizing Borges' discouragement should be interpreted as a sign of his determination to continue writing poetry. Indeed, "Mateo XXV,30" marks the beginning of a period in Borges' career in which poetry would again become his dominant mode of artistic expression.

The quality of Borges' personal life improved greatly upon the exiling of Perón in 1955. He was first named director of the national library and then professor of English and American at the University of Buenos Aires; the author was beginning to receive the national and international acclaim that his literary production so justly merited. These joys were tempered, however, by Borges' failing eyesight.

In 1958, Borges again republished his poetry collections—*Poemas 1923–1958*; he already had nine new poems to add to the work's "Otras composiciones" section. In addition, Borges continued to tinker with his previous work aiming for that ever elusive feeling of completeness and perfection. In this edition the poet deleted one additional poem from *Fervor de Buenos Aires*, gave minor revisions to twenty-four poems, and moderate revisions to three others—a total of twenty-seven revised poems and nine new ones. Thus, during the entire period from 1930–1958, the poet wrote a total of twenty-one new poems to be included in his *Poemas* collections and revised a total of one hundred eighteen previously published poems. The facts tend to dispel the myth of the "lyrical hiatus"; Borges' production of new poems may have slackened, but his interest in writing poetry never waned.

Among the nine new poems included in *Poemas 1923–1958* were four sonnets. The first of these "Una brújula," deals with the passage of time—the uncontrollable flow of history is written in a cryptic language by some unknown being or force. The poet expresses radical ignorance with respect to the riddle of life; human existence is an enigma, a game of chance, a secret code written by fate. The poet intuitively senses the hidden force that drives time's flow and compares its mystery to that of the forces that govern the movement of a compass needle. Like a watch's face seen in a dream or like the trembling of a sleeping bird, the compass needle moves—it is a metaphor for the human condition—men's lives, instead of being a free exercise of the will are governed by enigmatic forces that are beyond the scope of human understanding.

"Una llave en Salónica" tells of three Jews that were exiled from Spain due to the Spanish Inquisition. In Salonica—a Greek city where many Jews sought refuge until the World War II holocaust decimated their numbers—the key to their former house of worship in Toledo is still preserved. Freed by death from their hopes and fears, they can see the past mirrored—distant and fading—in the bronze key; it is a symbol of long, quiet suffering. Now that the door that the key once opened has been reduced to dust, the key has also become a secret symbol of dispersion—both the scattering of the Jewish people and the destruction of the past by the ravages of the winds of passing time. The key that endures is all "keys"; it is the same key that was tossed into the heavens and caught by the divinity during another incident of persecution during Roman times—it is the key of circular history.

"Un poeta del siglo XIII" may refer to Iacopo da Lentini who is said to have written the first sonnet. The poet's actual identity is of secondary importance as the poem's focus in on the creation of this new art form. Borges presents the thirteenth-century poet laboring over this new work unsure that the task has been well accomplished; he pauses upon the completing the work and faintly senses the future poetry that will be written in this form. However, the realization that the gods had chosen to reveal a new archetype through his own work was probably beyond this poet's comprehension. Borges praises the sonnet as a clear form that can capture all the mysteries and labyrinths that life holds. Like the world of myth that Oedipus represents, the sonnet is an eternal constant in a constantly mutating universe.

In "Un soldado de Urbina" the poet has Cervantes feeling unworthy of another deed that would be the equal of his participation in the glorious victory at Lepanto. The future author of the *Quijote* fled into a literary dream world—"Se creía acabado, solo, y pobre" (OP p. 162)—not knowing that he was on the verge of creating his finest work. This sonnet is extremely autobiographical—too modest to write about himself, Borges instead writes of an author that shared some of his own doubts. The poem's optimistic outlook—that the best is yet to come—marks the end of the severe depression that Borges had suffered from during the Peronist period. Borges' own life is summarized by two verses that he applied to Cervantes:

> Para borrar o mitigar la saña
> De lo real, buscaba lo soñado (OP p. 162)

The remaining five poems are all written in rhymed quatrains; Borges is now enjoying experimenting with more traditional poetic structures. The first of these poems—"Límites"—deals with the limits imposed on the human experience by secret powers that direct the flow of human life and whose exact nature is beyond man's comprehension. Humans are once again recognized as finite beings with limited possibilities. Everything has an ending; we do not realize all of the goodbyes that we are saying on a daily basis: there is a street that he will never see again, a book that he has on his desk that he will never read, some garden gates in the southern outskirts of Buenos Aires through which he will never again pass, a door that has been closed for the last time, a mirror that will never reflect him again, a memory that has been irrevocably forgotten, the sun and the moon will never see him at a certain fountain again, and he will never again utter a certain Persian poem aloud. Clearly expressed is the sentiment that he is leaving certain chapters of his life behind him forever:

> Creo en el alba oír un atareado
> Rumor de multitudes que se alejan;
> Son lo que me ha querido y olvidado;
> Espacio y tiempo y Borges ya me dejan. (OP p. 164)

The poet feels that his past is now being totally erased and that he is entering a new space—the effect of the poet's encroaching blindness can be felt here—in which linear time has ceased to exist.

The poem "Baltasar Gracián" bitterly denounces the Golden Age poet's work as consisting of nothing more than clever plays on words, ingenious but meaningless metaphors, and sophisticated form with no real substance to give it validity. Simultaneously, Borges is dismissing all of the avant-garde twentieth-century literary movements as basically frivolous and lacking real substance; the poem is also a condemnation of Borges' own youthful ultraist excesses. Gracián's poetry is deemed worthless because it is not anchored firmly in the world of myth, in the classics, or in religious and moral beliefs; in addition, Gracián failed to treat essential themes such as divine and human love. Borges then presents two visions of Gracián in the hereafter. In the first of these, Borges asks what the poet must have felt upon being forced to contemplate the splendors of eternal archetypes and has the poor Gracián lamenting: ". . . Vanamente / Busqué alimento en sombras y en errores" (OP p. 166). Borges then speculates that when ultimate truth was revealed to Gracián in all of its fury, perhaps the poet was struck blind (this ties into the previous mention of Oedipus in the poem and also can be seen as a hint that Borges' own blindness could be the gods' way of punishing him for the literary sins of his youth). Finally, Borges imagines a more likely scenario in which Gracián is never allowed into paradise, but instead is eternally condemned to revolve his empty games, plays on words, and "emblems" through the consciousness of his memory.

César Fernández Moreno criticizes this poem harshly calling it "unpoetic":

> No comprendemos por qué ha elegido Borges la forma versificada para expresar estos pensamientos completamente ensayísticos, casi científicos, irreparablemente prosaicos, en el sentido de no poéticos. Es éste un ejemplo cabal de verso sin poesía, donde el ritmo y la rima nada agregan a la expresión . . . [9]

Granted that this is not one of Borges' finest works, Moreno overlooks the fact that the poem itself is a parody of the bad poetry that it criticizes.

Borges' first poem on a Saxon theme is "Un sajón (A.D. 449)"; the poem could easily be called the mythical founding of England. The poem opens with the Saxons stepping off their boats at dawn. It tells of their difficult journey across the sea to settle in a new land, how they toiled long hours, and brought their traditions with them, including their pagan gods and primitive religious rites. They brought the seeds of the English language that would later flower into great poetry and they coined strange metaphors (Borges actually uses two of their kennings in the poem). In short, through sacrifice and hard work they gave birth to England. One of the elements that clearly most attracts Borges to the Saxons is their rich fantasy world full of magic and mysteries. In many ways, this poem repeats the basic themes expressed in "Dulcia linquimos arva" from *Luna de enfrente*; the poet has just changed the setting from Argentina to England.

"El Golem" is a long narrative poem inspired by Borges' adolescent reading of Meyrink's work *Der Golem*. The search for the secret key to unlock the mystery of the universe and the idea of creating another man by means of intense mental concentration are among Borges' obsessions; in "El Golem," he combines both of these themes. The poem is based on the philosophical premise that the name of a thing represents and *is* its archetype; if one were to discover God's secret name, one would become god-like and be graced with divine powers. Adam and the stars knew the secret when they were in paradise, but through original sin it has been lost. The poem focuses on the Prague rabbi who by using cabalistic encantations finally succeeded in reproducing aloud the secret divine name. With this power he turned a dummy into a man-like creature who became imprisoned—like real men are—in the context of space, time, and a fixed identity. The rabbi named his creation "Golem" and the poet backs up his story with his reference to Scholem's real book on the subject. After instructing his creature about the nature of the universe, the rabbi was able to put its limited abilities to work sweeping out the synagogue. Despite the rabbi's relative success, the creature was obviously defective—it could not speak and its eyes were more thing-like than alive. There must have been some fault in the rabbi's magic or a slight error in his pronunciation of the secret word that caused the creature to be defective. The rabbi regrets having created this monster and realizes the purposelessness of any effort to add one more symbol to the myriad number of existing symbols in the universe. The conclusion is that it was wrong to add another cause and effect—another dilemma—to an already overburdened world. The last quatrain abandons the hapless rabbi to his quandary and speculates about what God must think about the vanity and foolishness of such men. Borges again repeats here his basic message on the limitations inherent in the human experience; men who try to claim the absolute—the archetypes—as their own are doomed to dismal failure; they are damned by their own pride. Their sin is that of hubris, the desire of intrinsically flawed and finite humans to usurp the realm of the infinite. To attain happiness, men must know themselves, know their limitations, and be resigned to them.

In "El tango," Borges uses the medieval "Ubi sunt" theme as

a point of departure for a poem expressing nostalgia for the now lost world of the turn of the century "compadrito." The poet realizes that there is a bit of naïveté in the "¿Dónde estarán" question: ". . . como si hubiera / Una región en que el Ayer pudiera / Ser el Hoy . . ." (OP p. 173). The past no longer exists and to believe otherwise is to deny the truth. With this limitation clearly in mind, the poet nonetheless proceeds to use the "Ubi sunt" motif to conjure up the memory of the vanished Buenos Aires neighborhood toughs that always had obsessed his imagination. For Borges, the "compadritos" are modern epic heroes; they are the twentieth century's version of the knight-errant, but with their own distintive idiosyncrasies. The poet is fascinated with these men who committed gratuitous acts of violence; no traditional motives such as hate, love, or money drove them, their violence was like a primeval instinct. But, sadly, the "compadritos"—like the knights before them—have disappeared virtually without a trace:

> Una mitología de puñales
> lentamente se anula en el olvido;
> Una canción de gesta se ha perdido
> En sórdidas noticias policiales. (OP p. 174)

Nonetheless, like the knights, the "compadritos" live on tenuously in the songs the bards created to sing about their exploits: "esos muertos viven en el tango" (OP p. 174). With the aid of the guitar's rendering of the strains of old tangos, the poet can still conjure up memories of the "compadritos" dancing on suburban street corners. In the timelessness of an isolated instant the poet has briefly succeeded in recovering a bit of the past:

> En un instante que hoy emerge aislado,
> Sin antes ni después, contra el olvido,
> Y que tiene el sabor de lo perdido,
> De lo perdido y lo recuperado. (OP p. 175)

The tango music defies time precisely because its very substance is flowing time; therefore it is more durable than mortal men whose substance is also time joined to a physical body—which time ultimately degenerates into dust. For the poet, the tango creates a dark unreal past that somehow resembles truth; for him it invents the impossible dream of having died like a man while fighting on one of those pink suburban street corners (with the added advantage, of course, of being able to safely awaken from the dream).

In summary, these mid-1950's poems reveal a poet who is turning into a "sage" made wise by the maturity of his years. He has begun to understand some of the secret workings of the universe and how they operate in men's lives. He recognizes and accepts with resignation the limits of human capabilities. Above all, he is a man who knows himself; he has discovered his "aleph."

Notes

[1] Zunilda Gertel, *Borges y su retorno a la poesía*. (New York: The University of Iowa and Las Américas Publishing Co., 1969), p. 9. Hereafter cited in text as ZG.

[2] Emir Rodríguez Monegal, *Jorge Luis Borges: A Literary Biography* (New York: E.P. Dutton, 1978), p. 233. Hereafter cited in text as RM.

[3] Jorge Luis Borges, "An Autobiographical Essay," *The Aleph and Other Stories 1933–1969*, Norman Thomas di Giovanni, editor and translator (New York: E.P. Dutton, 1978), p. 238. Hereafter cited in text as AE.

[4] Rita Guibert, "Borges habla de Borges," *Jorge Luis Borges: El escritor y la crítica*, Jaime Alazraki, editor (Madrid: Taurus Ediciones, 1976), p. 339. Hereafter cited in text as RG.

[5] Jorge Luis Borges, *Obra poética 1923–1964* (Buenos Aires: Emecé Editores, S.A., 1964), p. 140. Hereafter cited in text as OP.

[6] Martin S. Stabb, *Jorge Luis Borges* (Boston: Twayne Publishers, 1970), p. 49.

[7] Emilio Carilla's article "Un poema de Borges" (listed in the bibliography) provides some more information on the historical sources of "Poema conjetural." A more bare bones account—but far more to the point—can be found in a brief note on p. 296–297 in Norman Thomas di Giovanni's anthology of Borges' poetry entitled *Selected Poems 1923–1967* (also listed in the bibliography).

[8] Jorge Luis Borges, *Selected Poems 1923–1967*, ed. Norman Thomas di Giovanni (New York: Dell Publishing Co., 1969), p. 315.

[9] César Fernández Moreno, *Introducción a la poesía*, (México: Fondo de Cultura Económica, 1962), p. 114.

7

The Maker's World

Borges describes the genesis of his next collection of poems and short prose pieces in the following manner:

> Around 1954, I began writing short prose pieces—sketches and parables. One day, my friend Carlos Frías, of Emecé, told me he needed a new book for the series of my so-called complete works. I said I had none to give him, but Frías persisted saying, "Every writer has a book if he only looks for it." Going through drawers at home one idle Sunday, I began ferreting out uncollected poems and prose pieces, some of the latter going back to my days on *Crítica*. These odds and ends, sorted out and ordered and published in 1960, became *El hacedor* (The Maker).[1]

Examples of *El hacedor*'s short prose pieces dating back to the 1930's during Borges' association with the Buenos Aires tabloid *Crítica* include "Dreamtigers"—which became the title piece for the English translation—, "Argumentum Ornithologicum," "Toenails," and "The Draped Mirrors." "Dialogue on a Dialogue" appeared in *Destiempo*—the magazine that Borges founded with the help of Aldolfo Bioy Casares—in late 1936. As Borges states, the balance of the other prose pieces were written as "sketches" and "parables" beginning in about 1954. As for the poetry, some of it started appearing in print as early as the late 1940's in the pages of *Los anales de Buenos Aires*—Borges began editing that literary journal in 1936. At least six of *El hacedor*'s selections—five poems and one prose piece—were published under imaginative pseudonyms in the "Museum" section of *Los anales de Buenos Aires*. When Borges chose this same title—"Museo"—for the section of *El hacedor* that contains these pieces, he publicly revealed the trick that he had played on his readers. (Thus, all of *El hacedor*'s poems were not written after 1958 as Zunilda Gertel states in her book on Borges' poetry.)[2] The fact that the texts written in the 1930's and 1940's blend so well with the 1950's texts—so thoroughly in fact that even more sophisticated readers are unable to distinguish between them—serves to prove the remarkable continuity and cohesiveness inherent in Borges' work.

Despite the cut and paste technique that Borges used to create *El hacedor*, the author feels that this work somehow turned out to be his most personal:

> Remarkably, this book, which I accumulated rather than wrote, seems to me my most personal work, and to my taste, maybe my best. The explanation is only too easy: the pages of *El hacedor* contain no padding. Each piece was written for its own sake and out of an inner necessity. By the time it was undertaken, I had come to realize that fine writing is a mistake, and a mistake born out of vanity. Good writing, I firmly believe, should be done in an unobtrusive way. (AE p. 253)

The following additional quote from Borges' "Autobiographical Essay" that refers to *El hacedor*'s "Epílogo" provides insight into why the work turned out to be such a personal expression of Borges' inner world:

> On the closing page of that book, I told of a man who sets out to make a picture of the universe. After many years, he has covered a blank wall with images of ships, towers, horses, weapons, and men, only to find out at the moment of his death that he has drawn a likeness of his own face. This may be the case of all books; it is certainly the case of this particular book. (AE p. 253–254)

In reality, all of Borges' previous works were drawing the lines that would make up the whole picture; in *El hacedor* the author added the finishing touches to a self-portrait that he did not originally set out to create. Miguel Enguídanos in his "Introduction" to *Dreamtigers*—the English translation of *El hacedor*—sums up Borges' self recognition process:

> His work—and by now it can be viewed as a whole—is altogether poetic, personal, the work of a spirit so withdrawn that solitude has

enlarged it and made him now see in that solitude the secret of the whole universe, now tremble before its undecipherable mysteries. Borges' "theme," then, throughout all his work—including his now famous fantasy narratives—has been simply Borges himself.[3]

Any doubt that the reader may have about this affirmation should be dispelled by the work's first brief narrative—entitled "El hacedor." In it Borges discusses two of his greatest frustrations in life—not having been born to be a man of action like many of his ancestors had been and the pain of never having been able to establish a lasting love relationship. The poet resigns himself to these limitations and finds that it is precisely his blindness that liberates him from these frustrations—freed from seeing and being confronted with objective reality, the poet is now freer to blend "reality" with his own inner realities consisting of fantasies and dreams. Enguídanos again concisely summarizes these concepts:

> The imprecise Homer-Borges of the story "El hacedor" knows very well that the weapon for combating life's final disillusionment, time's inexorable weight, and the terror and anguish of darkness, is none other than his capacity to dream and to sing. Dreams and song make the world bearable, habitable; they make the dark places bright. (ME p. 13)

Enguídanos also shows good insight into *El hacedor*'s preface in which Borges dedicates the work to Leopoldo Lugones, a poet that Borges had violently attacked in his ultraist days and then ultimately praised in his more mature years. Enguídanos sees the dream that Borges invents—in it Borges presents a copy of this new work to the long-dead Lugones who accepts it and even finds some merit in the book—as a way of exorcizing "old, malignant spirits"; with this symbolic act, Borges has liberated himself from the past by making peace with it. Enguídanos gives this résumé of Borges' motivation in writing the Lugones dedication:

> He wants now to incorporate into his book, into his song, the feeling that in his hostility toward the great poet of the generation preceding

his own there was somehow a great and heartfelt love. For without internal peace and order the poet cannot truly face the chaos of life, or manage to have his work's labyrinth of lines trace the image of his face. (ME p. 16–17)

With his past frustrations and conflicts resolved and put aside, the poet can now move foward with more assurance—unimpaired by the specter of the past—into his own reality, a reality forged with fantasies and dreams.

A good starting point to examine the poetry contained in *El hacedor* are the five pieces in the "Museo" or "Museum" section that date back to the 1940's. All of these pieces deal in some way with the limits inherent to the human experience. This is most openly expressed in the poem "Límites" which foreshadows the longer poem with the same title and theme that would appear in *Poemas 1923–1958*. The tone of world weariness is the same that dates back to *Fervor de Buenos Aires* and especially to *Luna de enfrente*. Men are constantly closing doors that limit the realm of their future possibilities; humans are finite creatures whose repetitive acts in daily life only serve as a reminder of their certain death. Despite the cyclical flow of history, the lives of individual men are relentlessly linear; living is composed of countless small deaths that symbolize man's final demise.

Supposedly written by a twelveth-century Moslem poet, "Cuarteta" deals with man's refusal to accept the inevitability of his own death. The rhetorical question that the poet asks himself (How can it be possible that I shall die like the roses and Aristotle?) makes the reader smile smugly at the poor poet's pride, an arrogance tinged with both ingenuousness and anguish; then the reader soberly ponders the unbelievability of his own death. It is difficult indeed to grasp the full import of one's essential nothingness.

Borges elaborates on this same theme in "El poeta declara su nombradía" in which the famous Moslem poet wishes that he had been born dead for he realizes that all of the fame and glory that he has attained among men is utterly useless and devoid of meaning. The Moslem poet has succeeded in comprehending the mystery of the substance of human life: life is a constant humiliation because men are finite creatures that must die no matter what their greatness; living is dying. Life is a constant state of anguish caused by the fear of the certainty of that approaching death. In this case, knowledge has made the sage miserable.

The theme of useless glory is repeated in "El enemigo generoso"; in the poem Borges invents a historical scenario in which the king of Dublin sends an ironic message to Magnus Barfod—the would-be conqueror of Ireland. The king of Dublin vows to defeat his adversary and to erase his presence from the face of the earth. The king of Dublin's "generosity" consists of his desire that his enemy fight a glorious battle in which he would participate with such great heroism that this would mark the culminating moment of his life—only to lose the ultimate battle and have his life reduced to total oblivion hours afterwards. Both the poet's and the soldier's glory are quickly converted to ashes in death's crucible.

The final piece in the "Museum"—"Le regret d' Heraclite" expresses in a playful and ironic fashion Borges' own basic frustration in romantic love. The name "Heraclitus" suggests both the fire of passion and the fickle whims of women that have denied him true love—just another limitation that men are forced to endure.

Of the remaining twenty-four pieces in *El hacedor*, ten are sonnets, nine are written in rhymed quatrains, and only five are in free verse. Borges explains this noticeable shift from free verse to regular verse as follows:

> One salient consequence of my blindness was my gradual abandonment of free verse in favor of classical metrics. In fact, blindness made me take up the writing of poetry again. Since rough drafts were denied me, I had to fall back on memory. It is obviously easier to remember verse than prose, and to remember regular verse forms rather than free ones. Regular verse is, so to speak, portable. One can walk down the street or be riding the subway while composing and polishing a sonnet, for rhyme and meter have mnemonic virtues. In these years, I wrote dozens of sonnets and longer poems consisting of eleven-syllable quatrains. (AE p. 250)

Although Borges uses his blindness to explain this shift, it is obvious that Borges was enjoying experimenting with different modes of expression; he had expressed his essential themes in free verse, essays, and short stories, and was now exploring more fully the possibilities that regular verse offered to him. Also, the regular verse in itself symbolizes the order and stability that the poet so ardently aspires to attain. The regular verse also represents a discipline that the poet values more now in his maturity—the free verse of the 1920's was a method of demonstrating his rebelliousness and break with tradition. Borges provides some more insight on this process in his prologue to *Obra poética 1923–1964*:

> Como todo joven poeta, yo creí alguna vez que el verso libre es más fácil que el verso regular; ahora sé que es más arduo y que requiere la íntima convicción de ciertas páginas de Carl Sandburg o de su padre, Whitman.[4]

The poet did not originally choose free verse because he thought it was easier to write—that remark is more testimony to Borges' basic humility—but rather because he thought that at that moment in his life the free verse would be a more effective means of literary expression. In his mature years the poet now feels free to use whatever type of verse he pleases, that is, the type that he deems to be most suitable to a particular context.

The poems in *El hacedor* fall into three basic groups. Three poems are eulogies of recently deceased friends, the balance of the works either deal with Borges' own personal life and identity as a writer or with one of the writer's favorite themes and motifs—the most salient among these, of course, is time.

The three personal-tribute poems are "In Memoriam A. R.," "Elvira Alvear," and "Susana Soca"; all three were Borges' personal friends and all three of them died in 1959. "In Memoriam A. R." is a moving personal tribute to Alfonso Reyes with whom Borges felt privileged to share part of life's journey through the dream of the universe. Borges praises his friend's poetry and prose and observes that Reyes was naturally at home while living in many foreign lands—more so than mythical heroes such as Ulysses. But in lines such as ". . . quisiste / Ser nadie para ser todos los hombres" (OP p. 204), Borges is speaking about himself as much as about Alfonso Reyes. The poet uses the poem's last six quatrains to speculate about possible forms of life after death—the contemplation of an eternal face or archetype, life in another world like earth but more "vivid" and "complex," or an afterlife that mirrors one's own memories. However, the poet concludes that death's mysteries are beyond the comprehension of the living; but, he expresses the hope that Alfonso Reyes, wherever he may be: "Se aplicará dichoso y desvelado / Al otro enigma y a las otras leyes" (OP p. 205). Rather than tears, Borges proposes clapping and shouts of triumph to honor this admirable life so well lived.

"Elvira de Alvear" pays hommage to a Buenos Aires society woman whose eccentricites and beauty had fascinated Borges back in the 1930's. Elvira had everything—beauty, fortune, an illustrious family past—and led a charmed existence as if she were on a magic carpet. She lost herself in life's labyrinth and in the river of time; finally, she had nothing left but "generosa cortesía," that manifested itself in her warm smile—that is how Borges remembers her, always smiling. The poem is inscribed on a bronze plaque in the Alvear family's pantheon in the Recoleta cemetery.

The sonnet "Susana Soca" commemorates a Uruguayan society woman, poetess, and patron of the arts who was killed in a plane crash. Keeping her distance from the center of life's fray she was able to capture the finest nuances aided by her delicate artistic sensibility. Borges compares Susana Soca's fate to that of "aquella otra dama del espejo"—whom the gods also doomed to a fiery death—in order to place his friend's death in the context of cyclical history. Susana Soca's destiny is not unique—it is merely the repetition required by time's cyclical flow. In this manner Borges gives meaning to his friend's death; he imposes order upon what otherwise could be viewed as a chaotic and senseless event, thus avoiding existential despair. The poet also ennobles his friend by giving her death a mythical quality.

Almost one third of *El hacedor*'s poems are autobiographical to a large degree; the poet draws a picture of himself—of his outer and inner worlds—at the close of his sixth decade on earth. "Poema de los dones" comments on God's irony in giving him the directorship of the national library and blindness virtually simultaneously:

> Nadie rebaje a lágrima o reproche
> Esta declaración de la maestría
> De Dios, que con magnífica ironía
> Me dio a la vez los libros y la noche. (OP p. 176)

Borges is now the master of books that he can only read in dreams; the infinite library is now of no practical use to him. The poet compares his dilemma to that of a king who dies of hunger and thirst amid plenty:

> De hambre y de sed (narra una historia griega)
> Muere un rey entre fuentes y jardines;
> Yo fatigo sin rumbo los confines
> De esta alta y honda biblioteca ciega. (OP p. 176)

Note how the poet projects both his fatigue and blindness onto the library; he who had dreamed of paradise as an immense library now slowly explores his domain with a blind man's cane while all the world's riches lie uselessly on the shelves. Borges sees something more than mere chance that gave him the same fate as his predecessor—Paul Groussac—who was also blind. Here Borges brings in the theme of "el otro"; Borges is the other man by virtue of repeating his steps, his fate—it does not matter that they are different men because by sharing the same condition they become essentially one and the same. Borges now perceives his beloved world through the thick veil of approaching blindness—his life and surroundings permanently seem more and more dream-like, like oblivion.

In "Los Borges" the mature poet searches for his roots as a clue to his being; he speculates on his remote Portuguese ancestors and how they somehow persist in him. Although they never shared his interests, nonetheless they are present in him in their own small way:

> Indescifrablemente forman parte
> Del tiempo, de la tierra y del olvido. (OP p. 206)

The poet concludes that it is better that they have been forgotten as individuals because now they have merged into the concept of Portugal and share the glory of its impetuous explorations and conquests: they are like the mystic King Sebastián who lives in the eternity of his myth.

Borges continues this train of thought in the related sonnet "A Luis de Camoens." Although history did not preserve the days of Portugal's greatest glory and time's passage dulls the cutting edge of real men's heroism, the beautiful illusion lives on in the literary dream world that Camoens created in his masterpiece. By calling the work the "Eneida lusitana" instead of using its actual title, the poet reinforces its relationship to the world of myth (myth is a superior "reality" due to its stability—the historical swords are rusted museum pieces whereas the mythical ones shine eternally like new). Implicit in this poem is Borges' fervent hope that some part of his own work will achieve the coveted status of myth, and provide him with a measure of immortality.

Borges follows up on this projection of his own inner feelings onto others in the sonnet "A un viejo poeta"—ostensibly about Quevedo. The sonnet describes an old, tired Quevedo too preoccupied with the creation of a literary world to see the setting sun and the beauty of the moon. Quevedo is so absorbed in himself that he does not even recognize in the physical red moon, the "literary moon" that he wrote about in one of his sonnets (in part because he was not even talking about the moon at all, but rather about the Turks). In the reference to St. John the Divine (whose visions fascinated Borges), in this portrait of an old man wrapped up in a literary universe of his own creation, and in fragments such as "Y casi no lo ves" (referring to the countryside around the poet), the reader feels the presence of Borges more than that of Quevedo. Borges feels as if he is leaving the world and withdrawing—like Quevedo—into a shell of solitude.

"Al iniciar el estudio de la gramática anglosajona" reveals a Borges in a totally different frame of mind. The poet feels refreshed and renewed by the joy of learning something new—it has given him new strength and a sense of purpose. Borges imagines himself to be a Saxon speaking this strange tongue some fifty generations ago; the poet concludes that although the words may have changed, the images they produce in the minds of those who use them remain the same. Nonetheless, by saying these strange Saxon words aloud, the poet feels that he has truly recaptured a fragment of a long lost past and actualized it. The poem ends with a hymn of gratitude—he is grateful that before death overtook him, he was able to experience this pure language and glimpse the secrets it has locked inside itself:

> Alabado sea el infinito
> Laberinto de los efectos y de las causas
> Que antes de mostrarme el espejo
> En que no veré a nadie o veré a otro
> Me concede esta pura contemplación
> De un lenguaje del alba. (OP p. 217)

For Borges, this discovery of the Saxon tongue is virtually a mystical experience; it is a road to new dreams and fantasies that will serve to populate his solitude with a few rays of happiness.

"Oda compuesta en 1960" is one of Borges' most patriotic poems; it clearly demonstrates the degree to which Borges has related his own destiny to that of his country. This "ode" can be seen as Borges' very personal version of an Argentine epic poem in which his homeland takes on mythical proportions. In the poem's opening section, the poet expresses the desire to establish a dialogue with his destiny using poetry as a medium—he is what the water droplet is to the river or what an instant is to time; nonetheless, he wants to preserve these insights in poetry's eternity. In the poem's long center section, the poet expresses his enthusiastic love for his homeland in a long list of associations—the pampas, the turn-of-the-century Palermo neighborhood he so loved, personal family references, and even direct recent political references (the "lluvias de septiembre" refer to Perón's fall from power in September 1955). In the third and final section, the poet concludes that this list is insufficient, for his country is more than the simple sum of its parts—land, inhabitants, history. The poet longs for the ultimate joy—the contemplation of the face of the archetype that is Argentina, known only to God. This archetype is necessary in order that the poet can understand the true essence of his country, and so that the country can have a definite, permanent identity that can be forever preserved in myth. In the last verse—"Oh inseparable y misteriosa patria"—the poet evokes the mysterious bond he feels between his own personal destiny and that of his country. The poem exudes optimism and confidence which in turn reflects the poet's new and more positive vision of both himself and his country in the years immediately following the fall of Perón.

One of the finest poems in *El hacedor* is "Adrogué" (the name of Borges' beloved summer haven); it is written in what the poet calls the fourth dimension—memory. The poem marvelously evokes the beautiful garden world of Adrogué, which for Borges represents peace, shelter, a place to think, read and contact nature, and to attune himself to the true essence of the things around him. Borges always took comfort in Adrogué's familiar surroundings: he remembers the childhood delight of seeing the world through red and green-colored glass, the stone lion's head with a ring in its mouth, and countless other small details. In Adrogué even time's flow—symbolized here by the dripping faucet—seemed slower and more gentle. The poet sadly realizes that all of this belongs to an irrecuperable past:

¿Cómo pude perder aquel preciso

> Orden de humildes y queridas cosas,
> Inaccesibles hoy como las rosas
> Que dio al primer Adán el Paraíso? (OP p. 222)

The loss of Adrogué is a loss of order and stability, and also the loss of a glimpse of the archetype of paradise that Adrogué represents for the poet. (Borges returned to Adrogué with Alicia Jurado at the time that the Hotel Las Delicias was being demolished; the fact that the poet made the effort to undertake this sad pilgrimage unscores the importance he attached to his Adrogué memories.[5]) The poem's final two lines sum up the poet's feeling of helplessness and radical ignorance in the face of life's mystery whose substance is passing time:

> Y no comprendo cómo el tiempo pasa,
> Yo, que soy tiempo y sangre y agonía. (OP p. 222)

In short, for the poet, man is flesh and blood mated with flowing time; man's life is a constant movement toward death.

The third group of poems in *El hacedor* elaborates on some of Borges' preferred themes and motifs—time, mirrors, tigers, the moon, men of action, and literary dream worlds. As one would expect, the largest single group of these poems deals with the flow of time and its relation to men's lives; the poem "Adrogué" with its more immediate and personal presentation of time serves as a good introduction and contrast to this series of time poems in which the setting is more theoretical and abstract.

In "El reloj de arena" (the hourglass) the poet muses on how time is measured and symbolized by the shadow cast by a column, or by flowing water and how time and destiny intermingle to the point that they seem like one and the same. Then the poet proposes sand as another method for measuring time—a method seemingly thought up to measure the time of the dead:

> Que parece haber sido imaginada
> Para medir el tiempo de los muertos. (OP p. 178)

But, the hourglass has fallen into disuse, and has become a dusty relic of the past found in antique shops; it is ironic that even an instrument used to measure time has also been destroyed by time and relegated to the world of "dead" things. The hourglass fascinates the poet since its two joined glass cones form their own mini-cosmos, a closed system that becomes a metaphor for the universe; the falling grains of sand become a metaphor for human lives that constantly repeat their patterns in cyclical fashion. In addition, the falling grains obviously represent time's flow—humans die, but the cycle of falling sand (time) continues infinitely. In the falling sand the poet gets a glimpse of cosmic time and its inner workings, which also allows him to gain access to previous time cycles and to remember things forgotten by history and previous generations; nonetheless, time ultimately erases all traces of men and their lives, and the poet faces the same fate:

> Todo lo arrastra y pierde este incansable
> Hilo sutil de arena numerosa.
> No he de salvarme yo, fortuita cosa
> De tiempo, que es materia deleznable. (OP p. 180)

The two sonnets that make up the selection "Ajedrez" repeat the basic themes expressed in "El truco" in *Fervor de Buenos Aires*. Here chess, instead of the card game, is the ritual which defies time by becoming atemporal by dint of its endless repetitions, in stark contrast to individual men whose fate is oblivion.

> Cuando los jugadores se hayan ido,
> Cuando el tiempo los haya consumido,
> Ciertamente no habrá cesado el rito. (OP p. 181)

The game is a closed system, a dream world apart from reality, man's way of seeking order and regular rhythms in a chaotic universe.

The second sonnet devoted to the chess game develops a related theme—the cycle within a cycle within a cycle and so on to infinity. The pieces on the chess board do not know that they are being manipulated by men who control their destinies; in turn men are also being manipulated as the pawns of God's cosmic chess game, and in turn some other god or force manipulates God's cosmic chess game. The reference in the sonnet to "Omar" is the poet's way of letting the reader know of his immediate literary source for this piece—the *Rubáiyát* of Omar Khayyám in which the chess game is used as a metaphor for the human condition.

In the sonnet "Lluvia," the rain is the recurring cycle that becomes the poet's metaphor for the passage of time. The rain—and all such cyclical activities—can be used to recapture the primeval past (symbolized here by the freshness of the first rose). Borges uses the rain's cycle to recapture some of his own personal past—the security of his childhood home, the patio, and his deceased father's assuring voice. In short, the poet has discovered the key to one of life's mysteries: all rituals or cyclical activities are ways of recovering segments of past time—past cycles—that are now lost.

A statue of one of Cromwell's captains—whose lack of a precise name emphasizes his essential nothingness—serves as the point of departure for the sonnet "A la efigie de un capitán de los ejércitos de Cromwell." The image still has his hand on his sword as if the glorious battles of the past were ongoing enterprises requiring his valor. The statue allows the poet to conjure up briefly visions of the battles in the green English countryside that so characterized those troubled times; but, the swords of the captain's enemies are rusted and forgotten just as the arms of contemporary men will someday be. The message is clear and concise: men are ephemeral, glory among men is a useless trinket, and time is the true victor of all men's battles.

"Mil novecientos veintitantos" deals with historical time's circular flow whose sweep men living in their illusion of eternal present steadfastly refuse to see:

> Nos creíamos desterrados a un tiempo exhausto,
> El tiempo en el que nada puede ocurrir. (OP p. 208)

Men refuse to see that history's patterns are not infinite, and must eventually repeat themselves. The poet cites his own and his contemporaries' blindness to history's inevitable course while he and the others lost themselves in their daily routines. They could not even guess at the terrible moments history had in store for the world during World War II, nor could they imagine back in the calm and prosperous 1920's the tumultuous and ruinous course of Argentine history, nor understand why one day they would all be out in the streets yelling "Córdoba" (where the successful rebellion against Perón broke out in 1955). The poet concludes that despite history's cyclical nature, the foretelling of how and when it will weave one of its multitude of variations is beyond the capability of human understanding.

Three of *El hacedor*'s sonnets are devoted to Borges' fascination with the mystique of the "man of action." "Blind Pew" can be seen as a "generic" presentation of the anti-hero, and the fact that the bucaneer Pew was also blind makes him an appropriate choice to reflect Borges' own preoccupation with blindness. In this sonnet, the once glorious man of adventure is reduced to nothingness—he is poor, blind, broken in spirit, forgotten, chased by dogs, and the butt of the street urchin's ridicule. His misery was attenuated only by his memories of better days that held two treasures—secretly buried treasure and the legacy of death and destruction that he had wrought. The poet presents a more contemporary version of this same "man of action" theme in "Alusión a una sombra de mil ochocientos noventa y tantos." The setting is Borges' beloved turn-of-the-century Palermo neighborhood and the modern version of the buccaneer is the "compadrito"—in this case Juan Muraña. The poet uses the sonnet's last two verses to express the fervent hope that time will somehow spare Muraña's name from oblivion; but the poet does not fully understand what exactly it is that attracts him to these men who symbolize gratuitous violence. The sonnet's deliberately choppy rhythm adds to the dramatic, mysterious tone. The knife is the salient motif:

> Nada. Sólo el cuchillo de Muraña.
>   * * *
> El cuchillo. La cara se ha borrado
> Y de aquel mercenario cuyo austero
> Oficio era el coraje, no ha quedado
> Más que una sombra y un fulgor de acero. (OP p. 201)

Borges brings this "man of action" obsession closest to his own personal family experience in the third sonnet in this series—"Alusión a la muerte del Coronel Francisco Borges (1835–74)." This poem presents his paternal grandfather in a more favorable light than in the poem dedicated to him that appears in *Luna de enfrente* where the Coronel Borges is seen as a thoughtless object that is dragged from battle to battle, and to little purpose. Here his grandfather is almost deified in the eternal world of myth:

> Alto lo dejo en su épico universo
> Y casi no tocado por el verso. (OP p. 202)

Again, Borges chooses the man's moment of death as his point of departure:

> Lo dejo en el caballo, en esa hora
> Crepuscular en que buscó la muerte; (OP p. 202)

For Borges, his grandfather's life was practically the archetype of the man of action—a life whose daily routine was struggle and battle. This type of life is justified and given a purpose only as the prelude to the man's death, a death which the poet describes as both "amarga" and "vencedora." It is this violent and often apparently senseless death that defines the parameters that govern the man of action's life and give it its meaning. Pew the buccaneer, Muraña the hoodlum, and Francisco Borges the soldier become in essence one and the same man by sharing similar destinies.

The remaining poems in *El hacedor* each treat one of Borges' recurring themes—mirrors, the tiger, the moon, literature, and paradox. In "Los espejos" the poet ponders his childhood terror of mirrors—not only conventional mirrors, but also surfaces capable of producing a reflection such as water, shining furniture, and metal. The poet sees mirrors everywhere:

> Infinitos los veo, elementales
> Ejecutores de un antiguo pacto,
> Multiplicar el mundo como el acto
> Generativo, insomnes y fatales. (OP p. 184)

The mirrors reflect an impossible, "uninhabitable" space, a dream world that to the poet is more like an unquenchable nightmare. Whereas the poet's dreams are of his own creation and therefore controllable, the mirror's handiwork duplicates relentlessly the very reality the poet would rather forget. The mirror produces his double, threatening him, and creates its own dramatic theater world that he cannot manipulate. The poet is also upset by the mirror's mere mechanical qualities ("Todo acontece y nada se recuerda"); its reflections flash once and the mirrors cannot reproduce the images like man can do with fondly remembered dreams. Mirrors serve another perverse function: upon seeing themselves reflected, men realize that they too are mere dreams. The poet concludes that God created both mirrors and dreams to help remind men that they are mere reflections:

> Dios ha creado las noches que se arman
> De sueños y las formas del espejo
> Para que el hombre sienta que es reflejo
> Y vanidad. Por eso nos alarman. (OP p. 185)

Another of Borges' childhood fears and fascinations surges forth in "El otro tigre." While in the library the poet dreams up a tiger; his tiger is "Fuerte, inocente, ensangrentado, y nuevo"—it is strong, has a primeval innocence, is capable of terrible violent acts, and is always "new" like an archetype. The poet's tiger is also frighteningly real:

> Entre las rayas del bambú descifro

> Sus rayas y presiento la osatura
> Bajo la piel espléndida que vibra. (OP p. 197)

Nonetheless, the poet is unhappy with his handiwork, because he realizes that his poem has merely created a literary tiger—not a truly real tiger. Thus, he tries again to create yet a third tiger—another dreamtiger—although he realizes that the attempt will be frustrated and suspects that his efforts may be just plain senseless. "El otro tigre" skillfully weaves together several of Borges' principal themes: the dream world as opposed to reality, creating another being with the power of the mind ("El Golem" immediately comes to mind), and a fascination with gratuitous violence represented by the tiger. For Borges the tiger is to the animal kingdom what the man of action and the "compadrito" are to humankind.

The poet's long hymn to the moon (it is one of Borges' most extensive poems, consisting of twenty-three rhymed quatrains) begins like a fable or fairy tale with a "once upon a time . . .":

> Cuenta la historia que en aquel pasado
> Tiempo en que sucedieron tantas cosas
> Reales, imaginarias, y dudosas, . . . (OP p. 189)

The poet tells the reader to be prepared for a long narration in which reality will be mixed with fantasy. The poet (perhaps ironically referring to himself) tells of a writer who undertook the mammoth task of composing a single book that would include the entire universe, but upon finishing, he noticed to his chagrin that he had left out the moon. The poet warns us that the parable points out the dangers inherent in the literary profession—"Siempre se pierde lo esencial." The poet humbly confesses that even this very poem will probably fall victim to this common error. The poet uses this starting point to begin his indagations about the moon. It is significant that the poet claims not to remember where he first "saw" the moon—either in the world of books or in the heavens. In any case the literary moons stick in his memory more vividly than the real one (although the poet does concede that he did share some happy but brief romantic interludes under the light of the real moon). The metaphoric moons of poetry now seem more real—bewitched moon, dragon moon, bloody moon, silver moon, mirror moon. The poet recalls that in his youth he felt obligated—like all poets—to sing to the moon, and expresses no regrets that his poems full of "marble," "smoke," and "cold-snow" moons never saw their way into print. Borges also makes fun of his youthful belief (and the credo of most of the avant-garde movements at that time such as ultraism and creationism) that the poet's task was to find the new and real names for everything in the universe:

> Pensaba que el poeta es aquel hombre
> Que, como el rojo Adán del Paraíso,
> Impone a cada cosa su preciso
> Y verdadero y no sabido nombre. (OP p. 191)

Nonetheless, citing Ariosto as his teacher, the poet came to realize that the moon represented a repository of dreams, of the ineffable, and of flowing time. The poet now respectfully hesitates to disfigure the pure word "moon" with vain imagery:

> La veo indescifrable y cotidiana
> Y más allá de mi literatura. (OP p. 192)

In summary, the poet concludes that the moon is just another symbol given to mortal men by chance or fate as a pathway to the discovery of their own real name and identity:

> Es uno de los símbolos que al hombre
> Da el hado o el azar para que un día
> De exaltación gloriosa o agonía
> Pueda escribir su verdadero nombre. (OP p. 193)

The purpose of "Ariosto y los árabes" (another unusually long poem made up of two dozen rhymed quatrains) is to show and then to lament the manner in which Ariosto's *Orlando Furioso* was replaced by *One Thousand and One Nights* as one of the Western tradition's principal sources of inspiration for the generation of fantasies. The first quatrain summarizes much of Borges' literary thought:

> Nadie puede escribir un libro. Para
> Que un libro sea verdaderamente,
> Se requieren la aurora y el poniente,
> Siglos, armas y el mar que une y separa. (OP p. 211)

The poet tells us that it is impossible to write *the* book, the perfect book—a goal to which he subscribes, knowing that its complete attainment is beyond human achievement. However, to write a reasonably good book the writer must present and somehow reconcile conflicting opposites—symbolized here by sunrise and sunset and by the sea that simultaneously unites and divides. The poet then attributes such virtues to Ariosto, who also realized that the writer's task was to redream the already dreamed: "De volver a soñar lo ya soñado." At that time, Italy's air was propitiously full of dreams (as had been France's and England's producing the legends surrounding Roland and King Arthur), and Ariosto succeeded in weaving them into illusory splendors ("ilusorios esplendores") and a kaleidoscopic disorder ("un desorden de calidoscopio"). The poet reminds us that literature depends on this effective mixing of reality with fantasy but warns that both worlds are equally false. All of Europe got caught up in Ariosto's fantasy realm until its replacement with *One Thousand and One Nights* which won over the West much more than all of Islam's armies. The poet first sings the Arab work's praises but then laments that *Orlando Furioso* has become a dream no longer dreamed in our times:

> Por islámicas artes reducido
> A simple erudición, a mera historia
> Está solo, soñándose. (La gloria
> Es una de las formas del olvido.) (OP p. 214)

Nonetheless, once in a while it still shines brightly when rediscovered by a sensitive reader—like Borges—but it then soon fades away again. The poem echos some of Borges' own concern that the popularity of works in their own time—like that of his own—can lead just as easily to oblivion as to lasting glory.

In "Lucas, XXIII" the poet develops with a different twist than in "Ariosto y los árabes" the idea of the clashing opposities that paradoxically form a unified whole. The piece is based on the irony inherent in the story of the thief who wound up in paradise just by asking for it: the same "candor" that led him to ask for and receive forgiveness was also the force that led him to lead a life of thievery and murder. The villain and the saint have become one by means of a paradoxical virtue.

In summary, it can be said that what the attentive reader finds in *El hacedor* is a restatement and a reelaboration of themes and motifs already common in the poet's previous work. Nonetheless, Borges is correct in maintaining that the collection defines to a large degree both his being and his art. In renewing his commitment to his few essential themes the poet has remained faithful to the 1923 prologue to *Fervor de Buenos Aires* in which he pledged to always put effectiveness before novelty; and as much back then as now in *El hacedor*, the poet always strove to penetrate the inner truths that surround the mystery of man's existence, and to avoid becoming overly entangled in sectarian trivia along the way. *El hacedor* is exemplary proof of the remarkable unity and firm sense of purpose spanning decades that characterizes Borges' poetry. Just as each generation of writers repeats the same essential themes from the illusorily fresh perspective of their own historical moment and reality, Borges has repeated and reelaborated these basic themes from the perspective of youth, maturity, and old age. In *El hacedor* the poet does not discover a new poetic voice or find a heretofore recondite personal symbol, but rather the poet leisurely strolls through his garden of dreams leaving some fresh imprints on well trodden paths.

Notes

[1] Jorge Luis Borges, "An Autobiographical Essay," *The Aleph and Other Stories 1933–1969*, Norman Thomas di Giovanni, editor and translator (New York: E.P. Dutton, 1978), p. 253. Hereafter cited in text as AE.

[2] Zunilda Gertel, *Borges y su retorno a la poesía*. (New York: The University of Iowa and Las Américas Publishing Co., 1969), p. 132.

[3] Miguel Enguídanos, "Introduction," *Dreamtigers*, Jorge Luis Borges (Austin: University of Texas Press, 1964), p. 12. Hereafter cited in text as ME.

[4] Jorge Luis Borges, *Obra poética 1923–1964* (Buenos Aires: Emecé Editores, S.A., 1964), p. 12. Hereafter cited in text as OP.

[5] Alicia Jurado, *Genio y figura de Jorges Luis Borges* (Buenos Aires: Editorial universitaria, 1964), p. 20.

8

Borges' poetry 1960–1964

Three years after winning the Formentor prize in 1961, which marked the beginning of the process that would catapult him into the role of an internationally recognized literary superstar, Borges published his poetry collections again—*Obra poética 1923–1964*—and added twenty-nine new poems to his previous work. This proved to be the edition in which many new readers discovered Borges' poetry, since prior to the 1960's Borges' poetry had attracted only a very select readership. In *Obra poética 1923–1964*, the poet's penchant for constant revisions and refinements of previously written texts is still clearly in evidence. Borges decided to delete one additional poem from *Fervor de Buenos Aires* and to give minor revisions to thirty-five poems, moderate revisions to twenty-three poems, and extensive revisions to two poems—a total of sixty revised texts. The bulk of the revisions (thirty-seven) occurred in his first two poetry collections—*Fervor de Buenos Aires* and *Luna de enfrente*.

Of the twenty-nine new poems included in *Obra poética 1923–1964*, nineteen are sonnets and the bulk of the remaining ten texts are written in free verse. Again, Borges is obviously enjoying experimenting with the sonnet; its rigid structure and internal order mesh well with what the poet has to communicate. The poet now sees the algebra and the ritualistic games that had always fascinated him mirrored in the sonnet's rigors. The basic theme the new poems treat is the same—Borges himself and his personal, esthetic, and philosophical preoccupations. As would be expected, such themes as time, memory, history, and the "other," are generously represented. However, the majority of the poems—even those seemingly devoted to such diverse men as Spinoza, Milton, and Poe—are very clearly about the poet himself. Borges uses these poems to evaluate his basic ideas, the events in his life, and the quality of his own work; he includes a hymn of thanks for all the bountiful gifts that life has given him and even writes his own elegy, as if he were already dead and writing from the hereafter. Although the poet was destined to write many additional poems, these new poems added to *Obra poética 1923–1964* carry the stamp of completeness, a sense that the poet has finished delineating the circumference of the circle of his existence and has returned to the beginning. Here the poet puts in place the last piece that completes the puzzle; his career may go on, but the poet feels that the essential core of his work has been definitively and irrevocably realized and that what he has accomplished now belongs to history and memory.

Several texts deal with the concept of cyclical time evidenced by constantly repeated historical patterns. In "Milonga de dos hermanos" the guitar music conjures up dreams; the performer feels a story from the past being brought back by the night. The tale that follows is that of the Iberra brothers; the older brother kills his younger brother merely because the latter had more killings to his credit, and the older brother wanted to even up the score. The poet sums up the process in the last two verses:

> Es la historia de Caín
> Que sigue matando a Abel.[1]

The first two lines summarize the theme to be developed:

> Según su costumbre, el sol
> Brilla y muere, muere y brilla (OP p. 236)

But, passing time destroys all things:

> Se acabaron los valientes
> Y no han dejado semilla. (OP p. 237)

The poet then applies the "Ubi sunt?" theme to Argentine

history asking what has become of the early settlers and where are the warriors that fought the country's revolutions. Again, Borges replaces the knights-errant with the "compadrito." At this point, a voice—the collective consciousness—provides the consoling news that the past's heroes will continue to exist in the memory of future generations just as those now living will also be remembered. Besides, the ironic conclusion is that people are usually seen more favorably in retrospect:

> No hay cosa como la muerte
> Para mejorar la gente. (OP p. 237)

In addition, it does not matter very much what has happened to the heroes of the past because in any case, there will always be new ones in a never-ending cycle. The individual hero's fate is clear:

> A todos los gastó el tiempo,
> A todos los tapa el barro. (OP p. 238)

But, despite time's ravishes, the cycle continues onward unbroken. The poem ends with the universal consciousness again speaking the same words as before; thus, the poem's structure is also cyclical, and the ideas it expresses are the cyclical repetition of the medieval "Ubi sunt?" poems. In this manner, the poem itself is also a representation of the concepts that it expresses.

Time's cyclical flow is again the theme of the sonnet "Juan, I, 14." The Islamic ruler Harún, wishing to escape from his tedious existence amid countless splendors, left his palace in disguise to mingle with the common people and to savour and to suffer their human experience. The poet then actualizes the story using the word "today" ("Hoy"), and proceeds to tell Christ's life story as if it had not yet happened. This is not so much a reversal of the flow of historical time as a repetition of it: Christ's life-story occurred, then the Islamic ruler relived it, then Christ repeats his fate in modern times, and so on to infinity.

The sonnet "Edipo y el enigma" proposes an answer to the enigma of why men's lives flow in time to their inevitable destruction. The mythical sphinx saw man simultaneously in all phases of his life—childhood, maturity, and old age; to the sphinx (or to God) man is a linear succession whose existence in time is visible as a unified whole. Upon solving the sphinx's riddle, Oedipus sees a glimpse of the totality of his own being—a terrifying revelation. This is a vision not meant to be seen by ordinary mortals, who in their limited capacity of comprehension would be overwhelmed and destroyed if confronted with all of these three aspects of their being simultaneously. The poet is clear; all men are necessarily blind like Oedipus:

> Somos Edipo y de un eterno modo
> La larga y triple bestia somos, todo
> lo que seremos y lo que hemos sido. (OP p. 253)

A possible solution to time's riddle emerges: God mercifully provided a linear flow of time for the individual lives of mortal men coupled with the power to forget in order to protect mankind from the self-destructive effect of a holistic view of their being.

Cyclical time can also be seen in the mention of Cain in the sonnet entitled "El." The reader finds out in verse thirteen that Cain is actually the poem's narrator in the laconic sentence: "Me llamaban Caín" (OP p. 234). The use of the Spanish imperfect tense here—"they used to call me Caín"—carries with it the connotation that Cain has had many other names during history's cyclical flow. However, the poem's main theme is pantheism: the poet sees the presence of god everywhere—one tiny particle not only implies the whole but actually is the whole. God was not content with merely creating the universe; he is all of the things in the universe:

> No le basta crear. Es cada una
> De las criaturas de Su extraño mundo (OP p. 234)

If this is so, the conclusion is that by being everything God has also tasted the fires of hell by being Cain.

Two related sonnets—"Everness" and "Ewigkeit"—deal with the theme of a universal memory that preserves everything that has ever happened. "Everness" was in part inspired by the work of John Wilkins—a seventeenth-century inventor of a universal philosophical language. The poet maintains that total forgetting does not exist due to the existence of a universal memory that holds everything—past, present, and future:

> Y todo es una parte del diverso
> Cristal de esa memoria, el universo; (OP p. 251)

This concentrated poem comes to several other conclusions: the universe is infinite, time's flow cannot be checked, and only after death can man see the archetypes and "splendors." In the related sonnet "Ewigkeit"—German for eternity—the poet maintains that his verses are merely repeating the same themes and patterns that have come down through the ages in an endless cycle. Although he sees life as ephemeral and death as inevitable, for the poet this does not negate all the cherished things in his life because there is no total oblivion. All that the poet has experienced in life, even those things that his own memory has lost, lives on eternally in the universal memory:

> Sé que en la eternidad perdura y arde
> Lo mucho y lo precioso que he perdido (OP p. 252)

Three sonnets deal with the theme of "the other." In the first of these, appropriately entitled "El otro," the poet makes the point that it is really "the other" that really writes all literature; here "the other" can be seen as being the muse that inspires all literature. The poet cites Homer and the *Bible* as examples that lead to his conclusion:

> Sabía que otro—un Dios—es el que hiere
> De brusca luz nuestra labor oscura; (OP p. 225)

But, the muse often acts in mysterious ways, making Milton

blind (along with Borges) and Cervantes forgotten in his old age. The memory that remains in time belongs to the muse—the writer himself is reduced to nothingness.

"Alexander Selkirk" and "Odisea, Libro Vigésimo Tercero" are really the same sonnet with different external trappings. In "Alexander Selkirk" the protagonist dreams that he is still lost at sea—where he spent five years adrift—until the sound of the church bells remind him that he is back home in the English countryside; he spends his days reweaving his odyssey in his mind and telling it to whomever will listen in the local taverns. Although he is no longer the one who looked seemingly endlessly at the expanse of the sea, the "other" man—the lost one—still exists. The protagonist speculates as to whether his "other" knows that he is now safe in England among his own people. "Odisea, Libro Vigésimo Tercero" virtually duplicates the previous sonnet with the exception that Ulysses is now the protagonist who upon returning home asks the same question:

> . . . ¿dónde está aquel hombre
> Que en los días y noches del destierro
> Erraba por el mundo como un perro
> Y decía que Nadie era su nombre? (OP p. 233)

Several themes converge here. Most obvious is the "other" theme—in both of these sonnets the "other" of one's past persists somehow in the universal memory. Also present is the theme of one man as all men—Alexander Selkirk is Ulysses; Ulysses by calling himself "no one" has become everyone. Finally, the poet is restating his concept of circular history in which certain life configurations endlessly repeat themselves.

Two poems—"España" and "Sarmiento" have historical connotations. In "España" the poet tries to resolve his ambivalent feelings about Spain—it is clearly a love-hate relationship. Spain is present in the poet; he can do nothing about this fate, it is a given that he must accept "incesante y fatal." He lists a chronology of Spanish history based on the many peoples who have at some time invaded or occupied the Iberian peninsula. He lists the negative aspects of Spain along with the positive;

among the positive aspects he includes meaningful friendships, patios, and men of action and ideals. The poet concludes that modern Argentina is a product of this undeniable past:

> podemos profesar otros amores,
> podemos olvidarte
> como olvidamos nuestro propio pasado,
> porque inseparablemente estás en nosotros,
> en los íntimos hábitos de la sangre, (OP p. 256)

The past can be ignored, but that does not diminish its persistent presence preserved in the memory of the universe.

The purpose of the poem "Sarmiento" is to convert the historical man Sarmiento into a timeless myth; therefore, Sarmiento is given the god-like power to see the past, present and future simultaneously. By turning Sarmiento into a myth, the poet puts him beyond the manipulative powers of dictators and others who would use the great man's symbol to their own ends. Sarmiento is a persisting witness to Argentine history; he sees all—"nuestra infamia y nuestra gloria." He continues Argentina's struggle to comprehend its destiny and identity: "Es alguien / Que sigue odiando, amando y combatiendo" (OP p. 239). Sarmiento's faithful presence can be perceived at key junctures in his nation's history—such as the days when Perón fell from power. The last four verses are the key to the poem:

> En su larga visión como en un mágico
> Cristal que a un tiempo encierra las tres caras
> Del tiempo que es después, antes, ahora,
> Sarmiento el soñador sigue soñándonos. (OP p. 240)

Sarmiento, by still dreaming of Argentina, still helps to shape its current reality which in turn is also a dream.

"Fragmento" stands alone as an exercise that Borges undertook inspired by a poem by the Bolivian poet Ricardo Freyre in which the poet produced beautiful "word music" without any particular meaning. Borges explains: "Using a quite different theme, I tried to do something in free verse. I have worked in a number of Saxon and Old Norse kennings."[2] In this "fragment" the poet traces how a sword is passed through the generations to ultimately wind up in the hands of Beowulf at a key juncture in time. Implicit is the idea that one sword is all swords, the sword acquires mythical qualities from being forged in the dawn's cold and being inscribed with indecipherable writings. Borges' experiment works well in large measure due to the almost maddening repetition of the phrase "una espada." It becomes a magical encantation, creating a dramatic tone, speeding up the rhythm and creating a crescendo effect that carries the poem to its climax. The poem's fast, smooth rolling tempo corresponds to the passing of the sword from generation to generation.

Nine of the new poems in *Obra poética 1923–1964* that supposedly deal with literature in general or literary and historical personages, really deal with Borges himself. The person or literary work mentioned is usually just a substitute for Borges—in a sense they are the poet's "other"—his "otro." In "Composición escrita en un ejemplar de la gesta Beowulf" the poet speculates as to why he is studying Saxon grammar without really hoping to master it thoroughly while old age and blindness are overtaking him. The poet feels that the Saxon words that he repeats imprecisely over and over again symbolize what he has done in his own works—a constant repetition that never attains perfection. In addition, the poet senses the presence of his soul that the infinite universe beyond quietly awaits—a presence alluded to by his current studies and his poetry:

> Más allá de este afán y de este verso
> Me aguarda inagotable el universo. (OP p. 243)

The use of phrases such as "Me pregunto" and "me digo" lend a very personal almost confessional tone to this sonnet.

Continuing the Saxon theme, "A un poeta sajón" refers to the monk who composed "The Battle of Brunanburh" (which took place in 937). The muse's ancient voice called upon the monk to write an epic; although he is now dust, by creating a myth he succeeded in forging a persistent present in which he will always dwell—thus he really did not live in "yesterday," he is always fresh and actualized. Here again Borges uses frequent repetitions ("tú," "que," "y") to keep his free verse rapidly flowing and creating a sense of dramatic tension. Nonetheless, Borges finally concludes that this epic, noble as it may be, is preserved today only by the memory of a few select mortal souls who take the trouble to read and study it:

> Hoy no eres otra cosa que unas palabras
> Que los germanistas anotan.
> Hoy no eres otra cosa que mi voz
> Cuando revive tus palabras de hierro. (OP p. 247)

Upon reading the poem's last section that is set off from the rest of the text, one realizes that Borges sees in this now obscure monk a mirror of his own ultimate fate—that of being saved from utter oblivion by a small number of devoted readers who redream his dreams. These last six verses sound more like an epitaph to be inscribed on Borges' own tombstone:

> Pido a mis dioses o a la suma del tiempo
> Que mis días merezcan el olvido,
> Que mi nombre sea Nadie como el de Ulises,
> Pero que algún verso perdure
> En la noche propicia a la memoria
> O en las mañanas de los hombres. (OP p. 247)

Again the poet expresses the wish that his personal biography be lost but somehow transformed into a form of panhumanism in which he would be no man and all men; his immortality would consist of a few remembered verses.

"Hengest Cyning" ("Hengest the King") is divided into the inscription on the king's tomb and a dramatic monologue spoken by the dead king himself. The key structural element again is the effective use of repetition (the conjunction "y" begins about one third of the total number of verses); the monologue flows quickly, with a terse, tense quality. For Borges, Hengest is the archetype "man of action" who led a whirlwind career first as a mercenary and then as a ruler himself after he killed the Briton king. His voice rings strongly and confidently: he has forged his own destiny, not allowing others to direct life's course for him, and he has been faithful to his courage and daring which are the essence of his existence. Borges has plunged Hengest into his mythical world in which all time flows together; Hengest is an ancient version of the "compadrito"—the eternal man of action that Borges had wished so fervently to be. The poet fantasizes Hengest to be one of his own ancient, recondite "others."

In "Una rosa y Milton," Borges desires to recover in its perfect state the last rose that Milton ever brought near his face; he hopes that the same destiny that made Milton (and Borges) blind will grant him this wish. The poet directly addresses this archetypical rose urging it to shine forth in his verses as it once did in Milton's hands. Besides the wonderful irony of the universe's most perfect rose in the hands of a man unable to see it, the sonnet deals with the ultimate purpose of poetry—to seek out and at least partially capture the few essential, eternal archetypes.

In the sonnet "Lectores," Borges uses Cervantes as a point of departure to speak about himself. Borges proposes that Don Quijote never left his library, and merely dreamed all of his adventures, and that they were really his dreams and not those of Cervantes; the novel itself becomes the dream of a dream of a dream. Borges feels the same way about his own life's work; he has spent his life in a library weaving dreams and seeking some unknown something that is "immortal" and "essential." He feels like a child, slowly paging through the book of life, dreaming about vague things beyond his comprehension. Borges' own work, like that of Cervantes is nothing but a chronicle of dreams ("una crónica de sueños" [OP p. 227]). The sonnet "Spinoza" praises the Jewish philosopher's work that attempted—like Borges' own work—to map out the infinite complexity of the universe—a universe in which the whole is and is implied by all of its parts. The twilight mentioned in the sonnet refers to death's approach; meanwhile, for the poet

Borges or the philosopher Spinoza, the outside world does not truly exist. The quiet men—feeling free from all restraints—dream a universe of their own creation—a "clear" labyrinth. In some of the more autobiographical lines, Borges claims to be unperturbed by fame or his frustrations in love:

> No lo turba la fama, ese reflejo
> De sueños en el sueño de otro espejo,
> Ni el temeroso amor de las doncellas. (OP p. 254)

Borges was always attracted to Edgar Allan Poe's work; he saw Poe as a weaver of strange dreams, macabre fantasies. In short, Borges saw aspects of himself in this man who was more interested in his own literary space than in objective reality. In the sonnet "E. A. P.," Borges claims that Poe used the symbols of death as the very substance of his writing but did not fear death. Paradoxically, he feared love—symbolized here by the rose—and the ordinary happiness to be found in everyday life. Borges muses that since Poe gave himself up to inventing nightmares as if he were in the mirror looking out on the world, perhaps he continues to create horrid marvels from the other side of death's mirror.

"A un poeta menor de 1897" is a biting satire of the generation of modernist poets that preceded Borges. These poets tried to leave some felicitous verses for the sad twilight hours, but their poems were bizarre, and Borges does not know whether they actually were successful in accomplishing any of their objectives. In fact, the poet labels the modernists as vague, and doubts that they even existed. In the playful conclusion, Borges states that since he is alone, he wishes that oblivion might restore the "light shadow" of the modernist poet whose only scant virtue was to have tried to sing the twilight's praises. Later Borges changed the date in the poem's title to 1899 in order that the reader and critic might notice Borges' own birthdate and thus jump to the conclusion that the poet referred to in the sonnet is Borges himself. It is the most light-hearted piece among these new poems, and Borges obviously enjoyed poking fun at other poets and also at himself.

The sonnet "A quien ya no es joven" can refer to any poet or any man—but the clearest reference is to Borges himself. Life has run its preordained, predictable course; the references to Dido and Belisario make the poet's own life just part of history's endless cycle. The poet wonders why he looks for news of approaching death in literature when the grave has its mouth yawning open at him, waiting. The mirror—the mirror of death's reflection—dreams him, but after his death he will be immediately forgotten:

> Aquí te acecha el insondable espejo
> Que soñará y olvidará el reflejo
> De tus postrimerías y agonías.
> Ya te cerca lo último . . . (OP p. 231)

The specter of death hounds the poet: even his house and street are symbols of his last days.

The remaining seven poems in this series of new poems included in *Obra poética 1923–1964* become increasingly autobiographical and more and more obsessed with the poet's own death. In the sonnet "Texas" which was born out of Borges' first trip to the United States (during which he spent part of 1961 teaching at the University of Texas at Austin). The poet sees a variant of the "other" in Texas—he sees the northern and southern hemispheres mirroring their realities of broad plains, horses, cow hands, Indians, and lassos. By relating the battle of Thermopylae with the battle of the Alamo, Borges elevates Texas to mythical proportions and duly places it in the context of circular history. Nonetheless, the change in geographic location does not change Borges' basic preoccupation:

> Aquí también esa desconocida
> Y ansiosa y breve cosa que es la vida. (OP p. 242)

The sonnet "Buenos Aires" sees the poet's beloved city not in its usual role as a place of secure refuge, but rather as a map of his own humiliations and failures; common landmarks shout

out his shortcomings. However, he still feels close to his city for there he has seen and felt the parade of human existence:

> Aquí el incierto ayer y el hoy distinto
> Me han deparado los comunes casos
> De toda suerte humana; aquí mis pasos
> Urden su incalculable laberinto. (OP p. 230)

With many moments of unfulfillment in his past, the poet now awaits death in the city where he will be buried; rather than love, what unites the poet and his city is a common dread.

The tone of "El despertar" is almost desperate; the poet awakes from sleep's dreams to enter again the tedious shared dream of reality. The present moment seems heavy; it is weighted down by mankind's long history in addition to the poet's personal history. The poet longs for total self effacement, he hopes that the afterlife will provide a total erasure of past memories and free him from his voice, his face, his fear, and his fate:

> ¡Ah, si aquel otro despertar, la muerte
> Me deparara un tiempo sin memoria
> De mi nombre y de todo lo que he sido!
> ¡Ah, si en esa mañana hubiera olvido! (OP p. 229)

The inspiration for "Una moneda" is a very ordinary event: the poet is returning to Buenos Aires from Montevideo on a ferry boat that crosses the River Plate. He throws a coin—"una moneda que brilló y se anegó"—in the river's murky waters. The coin can be seen as a metaphor for human existence: "una cosa de luz que arrebataron el tiempo y la tiniebla." The poet, after committing this irrevocable act, sees a parallel between their two destinies. He has already added his own destiny to universal history, a destiny made up of "anguish," "love," and "vain vicissitudes"; on top of this he has now added the parallel destiny of the coin which has gone to a "soft abyss." The coin is in time and in life's labyrinth like the poet is, but the coin is oblivious to it all. The poet experiences mixed feelings of remorse and envy for having "killed" the coin. The poet feels remorse for having sent the coin to a form of the hereafter in which it will no longer enjoy its previous function, and he also feels envy, because the coin can enjoy a sweet oblivion not yet available to him (OP p. 260).

In the sonnet "Adam cast forth" the poet asks himself if the garden of paradise was just a dream—a dream dreamed by God, the God that the poet himself dreamed up. In this sequence, the poet's (or man's) dream created God, God's dream created paradise, and Adam and his decendents on earth believe that paradise was actually real. Although the memory of "clear paradise" is now hazy, the poet believes that it exists—like an archetype—but not for his own enjoyment. The poet is stuck with the far less ideal realities of the here and now. Nonetheless, the poet does not give himself over to despair because he can content himself with two consolations. First, as an eternal, timeless archetype, the dream of paradise can never be destroyed and serves as a permanent solace and inspiration to mankind. Second, although full enjoyment of the joys of paradise is not possible, it is enough to have had a least brief glimpses or hints of it during one's lifetime:

> Y, sin embargo, es mucho haber amado,
> Haber sido feliz, haber tocado
> El viviente Jardín, siquiera un día. (OP p. 259)

Borges uses the poem "Elegía" to take stock of where he has been and what he has done; it is similar to several poems included in *Luna de enfrente* that have the same function ("Casi juicio final" and "Mi vida entera" are good examples). In an elegaic tone ("Oh destino el de Borges . . .") the poet directly addresses his own destiny to have travelled widely and have returned to the lands of his ancestral roots. Again the poet effectively uses repetition (here the linking is done with the verb "haber") to keep his free verse rapidly and coherently flowing. The mirror motif surfaces again here, for one of the items that the poet has done was "to have grown old in so many mirrors" ("haber envejecido en tantos espejos" [OP p. 257]). Here the mirror serves as a reminder of passing time—each time a person looks in the mirror, the reflection seen has already grown older. The poet also repeats (on two occasions) his disappointment at not ever having found a satisfactory love relationship. Despite it all, the poet balances the scales of the positive and negative aspects of his life and comes to the conclusion that perhaps his own destiny is not any stranger than that of other men.

Borges chose to end his new additions to previous poetry collections with "Otro poema de los dones"; it is a hymn of thanks that serves to round out the poetry collection and to collect the loose threads of the poet's own personal experience. In this long litany of the things for which he has to be thankful, constant repetition is the key link between the disparate items ("por," "que," and "y" are the chief linking words). Virtually all of the poet's favorite motifs and themes are mentioned including the tiger, the rose, fire, mahogany, eucalyptus, algebra, chess, the sword, music, water, the diamond, his homeland, favorite philosophers and books, evenings, mornings, and even one more reference to his joy at seeing Perón's fall from power. In the reference to "el idioma que hablé hace siglos," he gives thanks for the happiness he derived from his recent Saxon grammar studies; implicit again is the theme of one man as representing all men. Borges gives thanks for English and German poetry but significantly and deliberately omits mention of French poetry (however, he does include Verlaine separately). He gives thanks for oblivion which can blot out or modify the past: "Por el olvido, que anula o modifica el pasado" (OP p. 264). The poet gives thanks for the existence of poetry and sums up his poetic theory in four brief lines:

> Por el hecho de que el poema es inagotable
> Y se confunde con la suma de las criaturas
> Y no llegará jamás al último verso
> Y varía según los hombres, (OP p. 265)

The poet knows that writing *the* definitive poem—that would perfectly emcompass the entire universe is not possible for mortal men. Instead, each generation of men adds to "the poem" what their own perspective and place in history has to offer; each generation develops lesser and greater variations of "the poem's" handful of essential themes. Therefore, "the poem" is endless and has inexhaustable possibilities; it is an archetype that is meant to be strived for, but never fully achieved.

Finally, it should be noted that "Otro poema de los dones" has a very definitive ring to it; it is as if the poet pronounced these words from his death bed. The four initial verses are illustrative:

> Gracias quiero dar al divino
> Laberinto de los efectos y de las causas
> Por la diversidad de las criaturas
> Que forman este singular universo, (OP p. 262)

In addition, his mention of Frances Haslam—his paternal grandmother—who asked to be forgiven for taking so long to die, seems to apply as much to the poet himself as to his grandmother. Then, in the lines immediately following the reference to his grandmother, the poet gives thanks for dreams and for death which he calls "hidden treasures." In short, the poet feels that he has lived his life and done his work; he can now patiently await death with a certain measure of self satisfaction, a feeling of completeness, and a good deal of eager anticipation.

Thus, in the twenty-nine poems Borges added to *Obra poética 1923–1964*, the reader should not be surprised to find little or no novelty. Borges remains faithful to his small corpus of basic themes, always seeking to give them a fresh treatment, that added nuance. These poems also carry the weighty stamp of finality; the poet has run the course, his essential task is now done. All further works will seem like the appendices added to a long book—written almost as an afterthought.

Notes

[1] Jorge Luis Borges, *Obra poética 1923–1964* (Buenos Aires: Emecé Editores, S.A., 1964), p. 236. Hereafter cited in text as OP.
[2] Jorge Luis Borges, *Selected Poems 1923–1967*, ed. Norman Thomas di Giovanni (New York: Dell Publishing Co., 1969), p. 306.

Conclusion

Paul Valéry's essay "On Literary Technique" attempts to define the attributes of a "modern poet"; the portrait drawn can be used to depict accurately the poet Borges and his work:

> And this leads us naturally to a totally new and modern conception of the poet. He is no longer the disheveled madman who writes a whole poem in the course of one feverish night; he is a cool scientist, almost an algebraist, in the service of a subtle dreamer. A hundred lines at the most will make up his longest poems. . . . He will take care not to hurl on to paper everything whispered to him in fortunate moments by the Muse of Free Association. On the contrary, everything he has imagined, felt, dreamed, and planned will be passed through a sieve, weighed, filtered, subjected to *form*, and condensed as much as possible so as to gain in power what it loses in length: a sonnet for example, will be a true quintessence, a nutrient, a concentrated and distilled juice, reduced to fourteen lines, carefully *composed* with a view to a final and overwhelming effect.[1]

Borges is an outstanding modern poet because he writes with a unique understanding of the inner workings of the poetic process itself and of the special role that poetry plays within the realm of human experience. Borges realizes that all good poetry is composed of "algebra" and "fire." In each poem, the "algebra" of rigorous structure and logical intellectual content must be effectively fused with the "fire" of emotion. Creating a suitable form to unite the objective and the subjective (or the rational and the irrational) into a multifaceted but coherent whole is Borges' art of poetry. Structure or form along with style are very important, but they are mere literary artifices—they are valuable tools to be used to an end, but they can never be an end in themselves. The artist who gives top billing to structure and style alone commits the absurd act of confusing the finished, unified work of art with the basic mechanical tools used to create it; structure and style must be art's slaves, never its master. Borges believes that although both structure and style are key elements in all poetry, they must remain as unobtrusive and seemingly "artless" as possible—they are essential but should recede subtly into the background, ceding the center of the stage to the dynamic interplay of content and emotion. Borges' apparently simple style and structures mask a web of hidden complexities that are composed of the many layers of interrelated systems which make up each poem's totality.

Borges believes in the muse—a mysterious inspirational force—that provides much of the impetus for his writing. This belief is the principal source of Borges' pantheism, which denies the validity of the individual "I" or ego in favor of a collective identity in which the poet's work becomes the expression of the universal consciousness. If one man is a representation of all men, then Borges' denial of both true originality and "novelty" are logical extensions of his belief system. Other corollaries that stem from these basic premises include Borges' belief in the cyclical character of men's lives, of history, and of poetry itself. Poetry is eternal because it repeatedly expresses the essential intuitions and messages that dwell in the universal consciousness. In this manner, poetry must necessarily use only the most commonplace themes and metaphors which become symbols of the eternity of its simultaneous richness and poverty.

However, although the essentials of the poetic process are dictated to a large extent by the muse or a similar inspirational force, the poet is still a true creator—an active participant in the poem's creation and not a passive stenographer of the muse's dictates. Guillermo Sucre further clarifies this fine and somewhat paradoxical distinction:

> Como Novalis, Borges comprende que toda poesía reposa en una creación fortuita, pero ésta es buscada e intencional. Por ello, nada más

lejos de la concepción borgiana que la imagen del poeta enajenado que escribe sólo por raptos, en una suerte de estado alucinatorio. El poeta, para él, es el que asume y somete el misterio, no el que se le subordina. Frente a lo desconocido, el poet se reconoce, no se mimetiza.[2]

The muse may inspire, but it is the poet who writes the actual poem.

To those bewildered over such apparent contradictions in the belief system that makes up Borges' poetics, Sucre provides some additional insight:

> Cada momento de esta poesía—lo mismo ocurre con toda la obra borgiana—se debate entre múltiples contradicciones; en el sentido último que resulta de tales contradicciones es donde hallamos su línea de intensidad, su última coherencia. (GS p. 149)

For Borges, the poet's task is to seek order and hidden harmonies in the seemingly infinite chaos of the universe; it is precisely in the apparent contradiction of paradox that the sought-after harmonies are found. The poet establishes order by transforming diverse, conflicting elements into the necessary small fragments that comprise coherent patterns in a greater unified whole.

Although Borges does his best to deny the ultimate importance of the individual ego, paradoxically one of the chief motivations he has in writing poetry is to save himself from total oblivion. The poet professes not to desire the preservation of the details of his own existence, but rather he hopes for a more tenuous form of immortality—to live on in the cycles of history by having a few of his best poems survive in anthologies. The poet's search for order also is a factor that drives him to write, and leads him to seek the archetypes which become symbols of immutable stability in the universe's infinite chaos. The archetypes also clearly symbolize perfection, which helps to explain why Borges has spent a lifetime constantly revising and trying to improve upon his previous work (this process has also given the poet's work great cohesiveness). Although the poet resigns himself to never reaching total perfection, the very attempt to achieve this ideal gives his art its meaning and its purpose. For this reason, Borges humbly tells his readers that his writings do not really "express" anything, but rather merely "allude" to and "mention" things. By "expressing" a thing, the work of art would actually become the thing so "expressed," and thus would attain the impossible goal of perfection. Borges has wisely concluded that human beings who are by nature imperfect are incapable of producing perfect creations.

Borges' quest for order led him to search for the essential archetypes which in turn defined for him the purpose of poetry and of all literature: literature is a repetitive, ritualistic process through which individual mortal men seek a justification and a meaning for human existence. Literature is a search for unfathomable absolute truths which are manifested to humans in the form of signs and symbols; the use of such signs and symbols are the poet's way of attaining "allusion" and "mention" of things which are substitutes for the actual "expression" or the "possession" of the unreachable absolute. In Borges' poetic cosmovision the most important symbol is time; it is a representation of man and his human condition. Like time, men are in a constant state of flux; they are both forever different and always essentially the same.

For the poet Borges, literature has another key function: it is a form of happiness and pleasure in itself. The quality of the communication between the poet and the reader determines the essential in literature—the thrill or esthetic pleasure that each reading produces. The degree of pleasure is a function of the intensity of the "commerce" between the poet and the reader.

One thing that Borges' poetry deliberately does not try to do is to depict and comment at length on "objective reality"—especially in terms of the contemporary political and social aspects of that "reality." To fault Borges for this "shortcoming" is to miss the point: the purpose of Borges' poetry is to restore what reality has taken away from mankind and not merely to describe that reality. Guillermo Sucre supports this line of thought:

> ¿No es la misión del poeta restituir al hombre lo que la realidad le sustrae o le niega? En esa restitución le va toda su pasión, toda su inteligencia, toda su voluntad creadora. La obra de Borges no es sino el intento por rescatar el universo en sus formas esenciales. Sentimos también que en esa obra él dilucida su propio destino, su más íntima experiencia, la aventura de su propia vida. (GS p. 154)

The poet Borges, by seeking his own roots and his own personal destiny through the poetic process, is really carrying out a "generic" task in the name of all of mankind. Therefore, Borges' poetry cannot be truly labeled as being "escapist," because Borges—like Lévi-Strauss—sees man as escaping from myth and losing himself in what is commonly called "objective reality." The poet Borges believes that modern man has become caught up in a false world of technological gadgets and socio-political games in order to avoid confronting the essential problem of delineating a meaning for his very existence. In this sense, Borges' poetry deals with the true, ultimate "objective reality"; rather than to escape reality, his poetry represents an attempt to return to basic, essential realities that modern man has abandoned in favor of ephemeral toys and trinkets.

What the poetry reveals is not a cold, calculating, detached intellectual trying his best to befuddle his hapless readers with a confusing world of illusion, but rather a warm, sensitive, caring, and decent human being who seeks to lend a modest dignity and a sense of purpose to human existence. Borges deftly avoids existential despair by using the poetic process to forge order and harmony out of the chaos of the infinite universe.

From the vantage point of old age Borges the sage tells us in a nutshell all that can be expected from a human life on planet earth:

> I no longer regard happiness as unattainable; once, long ago, I did. Now I know that it may occur at any moment but that it should never be sought after. As to failure or fame, they are quite irrelevant and I

never bother about them. What I'm out for now is peace, the enjoyment of thinking and friendship, and, though it may be too ambitious, a sense of loving and being loved.[3]

In summary, Borges' poetry is best described as being "essential poetry" deeply rooted in man's mythical origins; or as Borges tells us: "For myth is at the beginning of literature, and also at its end."[4] Finally, in Verlaine's words, which Borges was fond of repeating, and which have now become an immortal cliché: "Et tout le reste est littérature."

Notes

[1] Paul Valéry, *The Art of Poetry* trans. Denise Folliot (New York: Random House, 1961), p. 315, 317.

[2] Guillermo Sucre, *Borges el poeta* (Caracas: Monte Avila Editores, 1967), p. 151. Hereafter cited in text as GS.

[3] Jorge Luis Borges, "An Autobiographical Essay," *The Aleph and Other Stories 1933–1969*, Norman Thomas di Giovanni, editor and translator (New York: E.P. Dutton, 1978), p. 260.

[4] Jorge Luis Borges, *Dreamtigers*, trans. M. Boyer and H. Morland (Austin: The University of Texas Press, 1964), p. 42.

A Selected Bibliography

Part A: Borges' Principal Poetry Collections

Fervor de Buenos Aires. Buenos Aires: Serrantes, 1923.
Luna de enfrente. Buenos Aires: Proa, 1925.
Cuaderno San Martín. Buenos Aires: Proa, 1929.
Poemas [1922–1943]. Buenos Aires: Losada, 1943.
Poemas 1923–1953. Buenos Aires: Emecé, 1954.
Poemas 1923–1958. Buenos Aires: Emecé, 1958.
El hacedor. Buenos Aires: Emecé, 1960.
Obra poética 1923–1964. Buenos Aires: Emecé, 1964.
Para las seis cuerdas. Buenos Aires: Emecé, 1965.
Obra poética 1923–1966. Buenos Aires: Emecé, 1966.
Obra poética 1923–1967. Buenos Aires: Emecé, 1967.
Elogio de la sombra. Buenos Aires: Emecé, 1969.
Fervor de Buenos Aires. Buenos Aires: Emecé, 1969.
Luna de enfrente y Cuaderno San Martín. Buenos Aires: Emecé, 1969.
El otro, el mismo. Buenos Aires: Emecé, 1969.
El oro de los tigres. Buenos Aires: Emecé, 1972.
La rosa profunda. Buenos Aires: Emecé, 1975.
La moneda de hierro. Buenos Aires: Emecé, 1976.
Historia de la noche. Buenos Aires: Emecé, 1977.
La cifra. Buenos Aires: Emecé, 1981.
Los conjurados. Madrid: Alianza Editorial, 1985.

Part B: Literary Criticism on Borges and Other Works

Alazraki, Jaime. *La prosa narrativa de Jorge Luis Borges*. Madrid: Editorial Gredos, S.A., 1968.
Barnatán, Marcos R. *Borges*. Madrid: Ediciones ESPESA, 1972.
———. *Conocer Borges y su obra*. Barcelona: Dopesa, 1978.
Barrenechea, Ana María. *Borges the Labyrinth Maker*. Trans. Robert Lima. New York: New York University Press, 1965.
———. *La expresión de la irrealidad en la obra de Borges*. Buenos Aires: Editorial Paidós, 1967.
Bastos, María Luisa. *Borges ante la crítica argentina 1923–1960*. Buenos Aires: Ediciones Hispamerica, 1974.
Bell-Villada, Gene H. *Borges and His Fiction. A Guide to His Mind and Art*. Chapel Hill, North Carolina: The University of North Carolina Press, 1981.
Borges, Jorge Luis. *Adrogué*. Adrogué, República Argentina: Ediciones Adrogué, 1977.
———. "An Autobiographical Essay," *The Aleph and Other Stories 1933–1969*, Norman

Thomas Di Giovanni, editor and translator. New York: E. P. Dutton, 1978. Pp. 203–260.

———. *A Personal Anthology*. Anthony Kerrigan, editor. New York: Grove Press, 1967.

———. *Dreamtigers*. Trans. M. Boyer and H. Morland. Austin: University of Texas Press, 1964.

———. *El hacedor*. Buenos Aires: Emecé Editores, 1960.

———. *Labyrinths: Selected Stories and Other Writings*. Donald Yates and James Irby, editors, "Preface" by André Maurois. Norfolk, Connecticut: New Directions Books, 1962.

———. *Obra poética 1923–1964*. Buenos Aires: Emecé Editores, S. A., 1964.

———. *Obra poética 1923–1969*. Madrid: Alianza Editorial, 1972.

———. *Obras completas 1923–1972*. Buenos Aires: Emecé Editores, 1974.

———. *Otras inquisiciones*. Buenos Aires: Emecé Editores, 1960.

———. *Selected Poems 1923–1967*. Norman Thomas Di Giovanni, editor. New York: Dell Publishing Co., 1969.

Bousoño, Carlos. *Teoría de la expresión poética*. Fifth edition. 2 vols. Madrid: Editorial Gredos, 1970.

Burgin, Richard. *Conversations With Jorge Luis Borges*. New York: Holt, Rinehart and Winston, 1968.

Carilla, Emilio. "Un poema de Borges," *Jorge Luis Borges: El escritor y la crítica*, Jaime Alazraki, editor. Madrid: Taurus Ediciones, 1976. Pp. 117–131.

Christ, Ronald J. *The Narrow Act: Borges' Art of Allusion*. New York: New York University Press, 1969.

De Milleret, Jean. *Entrevistas con Jorge Luis Borges*. Caracas: Monte Avila Editores, 1970.

Diez-Canedo, Enrique. "*Fervor de Buenos Aires*," *Jorge Luis Borges: El escritor y la crítica*, Jaime Alazraki, editor. Madrid: Taurus Ediciones, 1976. Pp. 21–23.

Di Giovanni, Norman Thomas, Daniel Hapern and Frank MacShance (editors). *Borges on Writing*. New York: E. P. Dutton & Co., Inc., 1973.

Doyle, Raymond H. *La huella española en la obra de Borges*. Madrid: Playor (Colección Nova Scholar), S. A., 1976.

Dunham, Lowell and Ivar Ivask (editors). *The Cardinal Points of Borges*. Norman, Oklahoma: The University of Oklahoma Press, 1973.

Enguídanos, Miguel. "Introduction," *Dreamtigers*, Jorge Luis Borges. Austin: University of Texas Press, 1964. Pp. 9–17.

Ferrer, Manuel. *Borges y la nada*. London: Tamesis Books, 1971.

Fló, Juan (editor). *Contra Borges*. Buenos Aires: Editorial Galerna, 1978.

Gertel, Zunilda. *Borges y su retorno a la poesía*. New York: The University of Iowa and Las Américas Publishing Co., 1969.

Gómez de la Serna, Ramón. "El *Fervor de Buenos Aires*," *Jorge Luis Borges: El escritor y la crítica*, Jaime Alazraki, editor. Madrid: Taurus Ediciones, 1976. Pp. 24–26.

———. *Ismos*. Buenos Aires: Editorial Brújula, 1968.

González-Carbalho, José. *Indice de la poesía argentina contemporánea*. Santiago de Chile: Ediciones Ercilla, 1937.

Guibert, Rita. "Borges habla de Borges," *Jorge Luis Borges: El escritor y la crítica*, Jaime Alazraki, editor. Madrid: Taurus Ediciones, 1976. Pp. 318–355.

Ibarra, Néstor. *La nueva poesía argentina. Ensayo crítico sobre el ultraísmo 1921–1929*. Buenos Aires: Imprenta Viuda de Molinari, 1930.

Irby, James E. "Entrevista con Borges," in *Revista de la Universidad de México* (vol. 16, no. 10), Mexico City, June 1962, pp. 4–10.
Jurado, Alicia. *Genio y figura de Jorge Luis Borges*. Buenos Aires: Editorial Universitaria, 1964.
McMurray, George R. *Jorge Luis Borges*. New York: Frederick Ungar Publishing Company, 1980.
Meneses, Carlos. *Poesía juvenil de Jorge Luis Borges*. Barcelona: Editor José J. de Olañeta, 1978.
Montecchia, M. P. *Reportaje a Borges*. Buenos Aires: Ediciones Crisol, 1977.
Newman, Charles and Mary Kinzie (editors). *Prose for Borges*. Evanston: Northwestern University Press, 1972.
Ocampo, Victoria. *Diálogo con Borges*. Buenos Aires: Editorial Sur, 1969.
Phillips, Allen W. "Borges y su concepto de la metáfora," *Movimientos literarios de vanguardia en iberoamérica*. México, 1965. Pp. 41–53.
Renard, María Adela. "Estudio preliminar," *Poesías: Jorge Luis Borges*. Buenos Aires: Editorial Kapelusz, S. A., 1977. Pp. 17–61.
Rodríguez Monegal, Emir. *Borges, hacia una lectura poética*. Madrid: Ediciones Guadarrama, 1976.
———. *Jorge Luis Borges: A Literary Biography*. New York: E. P. Dutton, 1978.
Stabb, Martin S. *Jorge Luis Borges*. Boston: Twayne Publishers, 1970.
Sucre, Guillermo. *Borges el poeta*. Caracas: Monte Avila Editores, 1967.
Todo Borges y . . . . Producción Revista *Gente*. Buenos Aires: Editorial Atlántida, S. A., 1977.
Torre, Guillermo de. *Literaturas europeas de vanguardia*. Madrid, Caro Raggio, 1925.
———. "Luna de enfrente. Poemas," *Jorge Luis Borges: El escritor y la crítica*, Jaime Alazraki, editor. Madrid: Taurus Ediciones, 1976. Pp. 32–33.
———. "Para la prehistoria ultraísta de Borges," *Jorge Luis Borges: El escritor y la crítica*, Jaime Alazraki, editor. Madrid: Taurus Ediciones, 1976. Pp. 81–91.
———. *Ultraísmo, existencialismo, y objetivismo en literatura*. Madrid: Ediciones Guadarrama, 1968.
Wheelock, Carter. *The Mythmaker: A Study of Motif and Symbol in the Short Stories of Jorge Luis Borges*. Austin and London: University of Texas Press, 1969.
Yates, Donald A. "Cinco años de crítica borgiana: 13 libros nuevos," *Jorge Luis Borges: El escritor y la crítica*, Jaime Alazraki, editor. Madrid: Taurus Ediciones, 1976. Pp. 293–301.

Part C: Bibliographies on Borges

Becco, Horacio Jorge. *Jorge Luis Borges: Bibliografía total 1923–1973*. Buenos Aires: Casa Pardo, S. A., 1973.
Fiore, Robert L. "Toward a Bibliography on Jorge Luis Borges 1923–1969," *The Cardinal Points of Borges*, Dunham and Ivask, editors. Norman: The University of Oklahoma Press, 1971. Pp. 83–105.

Christos R. Romanos

Poetics of a Fictional Historian

American University Studies:
Series III (Comparative Literature), vol. 7
ISBN 0-8204-0088-2   267 pp.   hardback US $ 28.00

Recommended price – alterations reserved

This text seeks to re-establish a rigorous dialogue between fiction and historiography. The inquiry is guided by the precepts of phenomenology. It formulates an approach in reference to the oral performance by establishing the historicity of the author-function and by defining the territoriality of the reading experience. (In this experience, the historicity of the author-function and that of the reader converge.) In its application, the approach paves the way for the integration of less known literatures, such as Modern Greek, into the field of comparative literary history. The rise and history of the Greek novel are examined in a comparative context. The fiction of Alexandros Kotziás, a contemporary Greek novelist, is considered in relation to other novelists prominent in the European tradition. The novelist is viewed as a fictional historian.
Contents: The text views the novelist as a fictional historian and deals with the historicity of the author-function, the territoriality of the reading experience, and the rise and history of the Greek novel.

PETER LANG PUBLISHING, INC.
62 West 45th Street
USA – New York, NY 10036

Joseph M. Ditta

Natural and Conceptual Design
Radical Confusion in Critical Theory

American University Studies: Series IV
(English Language and Literature). Vol. 9
ISBN 0-8204-0119-6   202 pp.   hardcover/lam. US $ 30.00

Recommended price – alterations reserved

Critical theory, if it is ever to rise above interminable controversey, must at some point in its self-elaboration be concerned with the problems of internal consistency. Psychoanalysis, structuralism and deconstructionism, and Marxism are major critical modes primarily because of their claims to scientific, methodological, and philosophical validity. Yet these critical discourses are beset by logical and programmatic inconsistencies: the psychoanalytic approach to literary structure is theoretically committed to the "reconstruction" of a phantom psyche; the structuralist and deconstructionist approaches share an inability to broaden linguistic theory into an account of literary value; and Marxist theory is plagued by a political program which takes precedence over its function as critical theory. However, by reintroducing the critical concept of intentionality, the conceptual design of literary structures can be elicited, providing a presently lacking focus for most critical approaches.
Contents: Literary Critical Theory: Psychoanalysis. Structuralism and Deconstructionism, and Marxism.

PETER LANG PUBLISHING, INC.
62 West 45th Street
USA – New York, NY 10036

Ion T. Agheana

The Prose of Jorge Luis Borges
Existentialism and the Dynamics of Surprise

American University Studies: Series II
(Romance Languages and Literature). Vol. 13
ISBN 0-8204-0130-7   333 pp.   paperback/lam. US $ 31.85

Recommended price – alterations reserved

Like the Kafka of one of his essays, Jorge Luis Borges imposes himself at first as a man of iconoclastic singularity, as a writer who, having considered and discarded seemingly all the "isms" of literature and philosophy, creates a world *ex nihilo*. Yet minutely studied, Borges, like Kafka, who under close scrutiny reveals subtle affinities with other literatures, exhibits an unmistakable existential strain. The analysis of Borges' existentialism, identifiable in his prose works not as an unitary system but as a philosophical premise, together with the dynamics of surprise, constitute the object of the present study.
Contents: Jorge Luis Borges and Existentialism – The Misleading Symmetry – The Dynamics of Surprise.

PETER LANG PUBLISHING, INC.
62 West 45th Street
USA – New York, NY 10036